This book is about the power of connection, caring, and core values in a successful team culture, much like the Warriors. Jerry helps me to pass on his "Win the Day" philosophy to our Warrior culture. His book is one to be read by every coach, athlete, CEO, and leader to help understand how to best build and sustain a championship culture.

Steve Kerr, Head Coach, Three-time NBA World Champion Golden State Warriors

Jerry's wisdom has helped guide me through my work as director of athletics here at Middlebury College. He has had a transformative effect on the team cultures of all our coaches.

Erin Quinn, Director of Athletics, Middlebury College

Dr. Lynch's innovative approach to the relationship game is profound, perceptive, and unparalleled in the world of athletics.

Quin Snyder, Head Coach, NBA Utah Jazz

Our team culture has truly been reshaped and remolded by the wisdom and guidance of Dr. Jerry Lynch, who is an expert and leading figure in the area of building championship environments.

Sally Starr, Head Women's Field Hockey Coach, Boston University

Jerry has had a profound positive influence on all of my championship cultures in the past 30 years. His leadership training and development of solid team cultures is unparalleled, compelling, and relevant in today's world. *Win the Day* is a gem that will help you to sustain a healthy culture.

Bob Hansen, Head Men's Tennis Coach, Middlebury College

Over the years, I have had the opportunity to stay informed by Jerry Lynch. His books have made a big difference in helping me and my athletes reach our potential in many ways, including culture development.

Phil Jackson, 11-time NBA World Champion Coach and Athlete

Jerry Lynch transforms the world of athletics into a sacred space in which to absorb practical life lessons and ageless wisdom for inspiration and success.

Michael Murphy, Author of Golf in the Kingdom

For the last five years, I have had the privilege of working alongside Dr. Jerry Lynch and teaching the "Win the Day" mentality to high school, collegiate, and youth sports athletes and coaches across the globe. This book may be a collection of wisdom from some of the most famous and successful coaches of all time, but it is much more than that. It is over 100 championship seasons distilled into an easy-to-use guide for coaches of every level. This stuff works! How do I know? Because I use it every day in my own coaching, and you should too.

John O'Sullivan, Founder of Changing the Game Project, Host of the Way of Champions Podcast

WIN THE DAY

The Ultimate Coach's Guide to Build and Sustain a Championship Culture

JERRY LYNCH, Ph.D.

Author of Coaching With Heart

FOREWORD BY

STEVE KERR

Head Coach of the World Champion Golden State Warriors

COACHES CHOICE™

ISBN: 978-1-60679-477-7
Book layout: Cheery Sugabo
Cover design: Cheery Sugabo
Front cover photo: ©Brian Rothmuller/Icon SMI via ZUMA Press

Coaches Choice
P.O. Box 1828
Monterey, CA 93942
www.coacheschoice.com

DEDICATION

I dedicate this book to the ancient Taoist sage, Sun-Tzu, author of the 2,000-year-old Chinese classic, *The Art of War*, one of the most widely read tomes among generals, corporate CEOs, and athletic coaches throughout the world. Sun-Tzu believed that the essence of triumph in battle is a team culture with unity of purpose, caring, and deep connection. As you can see, his work has been an extraordinary affirmation, influence, and inspiration for the writing of my book.

ACKNOWLEDGMENTS

If this book makes a difference in your life, and I believe it will, it will be due in large part to my having had such awesome caring and loving colleagues and friends. What you are about to read is not just my doing. As an aspiring student of the Native American flute, I imagine myself being a hole through which the breath of others wiser than myself flows in your direction.

I am very grateful for Dr. Jim Peterson and Kristi Huelsing and the entire team at Coaches Choice for all their vision and insight determining that the time was ripe for a book of this caliber and nature. Their passion and love for the content convinced me that they were the perfect home for my book.

I would not have been able to write this book without having had the extraordinary opportunity of being asked by hundreds of coaches and athletic programs at the professional, collegiate, and high school levels to join their journeys in creating strong sustainable team cultures.

My very first involvement with a sports team happened in 1989 with the University of California, Santa Cruz men's tennis squad. As fortune would have it, we won the national championship, and I was hooked. Thirty years and 115 championship teams later, I realize that I've learned much more than I have ever taught, yet there is so much more I want to learn. To all of those athletic programs and coaches who opened their hearts and doors to me and my work, I am forever appreciative, and without you, this book would not have been written. No teams, no book.

I write all of my books on legal size yellow pads in undecipherable script, unless you are Sally Vaughn, my loyal, enthusiastic, affirming office assistant. Somehow, she can read every word, unlock the code, and turn those pages into a work of art with perfect font, formatting, and editorial suggestions. I don't write a word without your help. No Sally, no book.

Then, there is my loving, dedicated, and devoted partner and wife, Jan, who wasn't simply the image of the faithful, patient spouse in the background, tiptoeing through the house, taking care of the chores, extending an ineffable aura of praise and support. While true to some extent, Jan has her own projects as a physician with a robust patient load. Yet, she still managed to nudge and encourage me, when I was often discouraged. Because she believed in me and this project and its importance in changing the status quo of athletics, the book came to fruition. No Jan, no book.

Finally, I don't want to overlook you, the reader. I am honored and privileged, after all these years and 13 books, to have others like you who still believe in what I write and what I say. With so much love, gratitude, and good chi your way, I invite you to join the *Win the Day* message.

FOREWORD

Steve Kerr

In the summer of 2014, a couple of months after being named the head coach of the Golden State Warriors, I traveled to Seattle to visit Pete Carroll and watch the Seahawks' training camp. I had always admired Pete from afar, and though I had never met him, I was anxious to pick his brain about coaching. For years I watched his teams – both at USC and in Seattle – play with an amazing combination of speed, discipline, and joy, achieving incredible success at the highest levels of the sport. In fact, the Seahawks had just won Super Bowl XLVIII in February in a demolition of the Broncos, running, smiling and laughing their way to a huge victory.

As I prepared for the very first coaching job of my life, I thought to myself, "I want the Warriors to look like the Seahawks." And while I knew that spending a few days observing Pete and his team would be helpful, I had no idea that the visit would help shape my entire philosophy on coaching.

The next few days were fantastic. I sat in on team meetings, ate meals with the coaches, and watched the Seahawks practice up close. Pete made sure I was a part of everything. At one point, he told me to stick my head in the middle of the offensive huddle and listen to Russell Wilson call the play to his teammates. I had an up close view of the best football team in the world at work, and it was fascinating.

But what I will always remember—for the rest of my life—was when Pete called me into his office on day two, sat me down and asked, "So, how are you going to coach your team?" I wasn't exactly sure what he meant, so I hesitated and replied "you mean like what offense are we going to run?" And Pete said "no, that stuff doesn't matter. I'm talking about what your day is going to look like. What practice will feel like. What the environment will be. How your team will feel coming to work every day."

At that point, I had put in a ton of work preparing for my job. I had studied successful teams, built a video library of innovative plays, visited with other coaches in different sports, and written down all kinds of concepts and theories that I thought would work with the Warriors. But, when Pete asked me those questions, I realized I didn't really have a plan yet. I didn't know how practice would feel, or whether the players would enjoy the process, or what kind of culture we would have. I figured that stuff would just kind of happen on its own.

That's when Pete broke it down for me and helped me understand the very essence of coaching. "Write down ten things that are important to you, when you get back to your hotel tonight," he said. "What are the most important things to you, personally, in your life? When you come back tomorrow, we are going to narrow down those ten things to four. Those four principles represent you as a human being. We are all unique, so your four will be different from my four. But, if you are authentic with your team, and your daily routine at practice and games and team meetings reflects your principles, your personal core values, well then, now you're going somewhere. Now, you're building a culture. Now, you're coaching.

I want back to my hotel that night and thought about what I had witnessed at practice that day. There was music blasting on the speakers. Players were competing in every drill, desperate to win every single confrontation. There was intense study, preparation, and interaction in the team meetings, which were all upbeat and led by various assistant coaches. There was even a basketball shooting competition before the team meeting in the auditorium, with a stationary basket set up near the front. This was a daily ritual, and Pete had me compete against their resident champion, wide receiver Bryan Walters. I lost. (Which I'm still bitter about.)

I walked out of that building feeling on fire, adrenaline pumping, excited about life, excited about the Warriors, excited about coaching. And that's when it dawned on me—Pete Carroll had built his team's entire practice routine around the energy, curiosity, positivity, and joy that defined him. His team was a reflection of him, because every day was based on Pete's values, on what was important to him. And the combination of that wonderful culture and an amazingly gifted roster had helped the Seahawks win the Super Bowl. It all made sense.

I went back to Oakland, with thoughts flying through my head. I already had an idea of how I wanted our team to look and play. But, in order for things to take hold, all of the concepts and ideas and theories that I was ready to throw at my team had to be crystallized into a core philosophy, one that would be reflected in our daily routine. The team had to feel my authenticity, vulnerability, connection, caring, and passion for the job and for my players and for our success. Ultimately, for the Warriors' core values, I decided on joy, mindfulness, compassion, and competition. Those were the four principles that were ingrained in me, that had been instilled in me, either through my own life experiences or through genetics. Those were the things that mattered to me as a person, and everything we were going to do, every day, would reflect those values.

By the time training camp started, my staff and I had designed a routine that we felt would elicit a fun, disciplined, fast-paced style from our team. Practices were relatively brief, but they were swift. Music blasted in the gym during warm-ups and shooting drills. Video sessions were filled with humor, as well as instruction. Our coaches took turns running drills and spent plenty of time getting to connect with and know the players and their families.

We knew it wouldn't happen overnight, but we felt that, over time, our players would feel our joy, sense our caring and compassion for them, and recognize our competitive desire, as well as our mindful approach to coaching. Furthermore, hopefully, if we were consistent with that routine, the team would begin to take on an identity that reflected those ideals. Of course, connection and caring, along with the core values, would help to solidify the culture.

I'm proud to say that over time, our Warriors team has had wonderful success, mainly because we have had an incredibly talented group. The culture that has taken hold is shown in Steph Curry's joy, in Draymond Green's competitiveness, in the mindfulness of Andre Iguodala, and the compassions of Shaun Livingston and Klay Thompson. It is shown in the brilliantly unselfish play of Kevin Durant, who wanted to be a part of a team that connects, cares for and sacrifices for one another, and has forged an identity of his own amongst this wonderful group of players. Ultimately, players determine a team's ultimate success. It is the coach's job to give those players a vision, to develop a routine and a pattern that is meaningful and consistent. As such, when those things come together, the results can be beautiful.

At this point, it's a natural time to segue into the book you are holding, *Win the Day*, written by Dr. Jerry Lynch. It is a book about the power of connection, caring, and core values in a successful team culture, much like that of the Golden State Warriors. It is a book that will help you to create, model, and sustain what championship teams, like the Seahawks and Warriors, do on a daily basis. Through our conversations, texts, and emails, Jerry has helped me to pass on the "Win the Day" philosophy in our Warrior culture. To achieve success in sports, I believe a team's culture has to be connective, caring, and authentic, one way or another. It must come from the heart and soul of the coach and the athletes. Jerry captures that important dynamic perfectly in *Win the Day*, his seminal project in a long, distinguished career in sports, and helps you to implement its guiding principles.

Jerry has written 13 books and aided 115 championship teams in 30 years of culture work at the pro and college level. I first met him during my playing days with the Chicago Bulls, through our mutual friend and coach, Phil Jackson. Jerry's books, *Thinking Body, Dancing Mind*, and *The Way of the Champion,* were an inspiration to me during my playing days and are now valued by me as a coach.

Jerry continues to inspire me with his latest work, as I advance my coaching skills and career, trying to make the best possible connection and demonstrate caring with my players which helps them achieve their ultimate individual and collective greatness. *Win the Day* is a book that every coach, athlete, CEO, and leader in any aspect of life should read to understand how to best build a "Win the Day" culture for a team's or an organization's ultimate success.

CONTENTS

INTRODUCTION

Rediscovering Our North Star

Until I understand where I am, I can't get to where I'm going. This is the value of a compass when we need to know we're going in the right direction. But we also have an internal North Star ... that little nudge that tells us if we are on the right path to fulfilling our potential.

—John C. Maxwell, Author, Leadership, Coaching

For me, that nudge is a set of core values that keeps us on track as a culture. My advice is to pull out the spiritual compass that I present in this book every so often and make sure you are going in the best direction on this journey in sports and life.

My purpose in writing this book is to make a difference in the lives of coaches and athletes, to change the status quo of sports cultures, and to offer an ethical, spiritual, and emotional compass that can inspire, empower, and guide others to believe that their lives can be something other than ordinary. It is a book about caring, core values, and connection, of competing and coaching with love in athletics and life.

As a philosophical base, I lean on the wisdom, teachings, and values of a variety of cultures, such as ancient Chinese and Buddhist thought, Native American tradition, and Western psychology. For example, Taoist warriors understood that the power of their honorable core values (included in this book) was greater than the power of arms. This factor is what the Chinese call *Wu Shi*, or the Warrior spirit, which is about being totally alive to experience your potential for peak capacity, using values they considered weapons of the heart. These core values—connection and caring—are our non-negotiables. They are our North Star. According to former President Barack Obama, "There are gonna be a set of core values that shouldn't be up for debate. They should be our North Star." Much in agreement with former President Obama is the CEO of Apple Tim Cook: "Your core values matter. They are your North Star."

Being a champion is more than simply winning on the scoreboard; it is about winning the bigger, deeper more meaningful lessons of life through the experience of athletics. Basically, coaches and athletes champion what I call a "Win the Day" attitude by executing the important little things they can control now. It is an attitude that asks and answers the question: what's important now?

Greg Mckeown, in his book, *Essentialism*, talks about how WIN is an acronym that stands for "what's important now?"—the "in the present" experience of the play at hand, rather than obsessing over future results or outcomes. You WIN by staying focused on how you're competing now and thinking about your game plan, not the opponent's, and concentrating on what I call the essential absolutes, all those items you can control … your North Star.

Win the Day lays out the essential core values of championship sports cultures. This book is a way to care, connect, and help unite others, embrace diversity, have each other's backs, be selfless, and work together for a common cause greater than any ideology or any one individual. It is a book to help build, cultivate, and sustain a culture of champions who "Win the Day" by practicing specific core values that we all crave. It is about rediscovering our North Star or conscious compass in a chaotic world and infusing those values into our nervous systems in order to experience extraordinary performance and a sense of equanimity with right action and a more mindful way of competing and living.

"Win the Day" means that coaches and athletes control what they *can* and let go of outcomes and results. It means to never give up, regardless of the score; never be fearful of losing, because it's our greatest teacher; and never let your opponent defeat your spirit, your commitment to winning the day. It is about physical, emotional, spiritual, and mental preparation and doing the little important things brilliantly in the present moment, rather than the big things marginally in the future. It's all about "what's important now" (WIN) in order to Win the Day.

I combine the body of work I have created with 115 championship cultures in the hope of changing the world of sports as we know it, while inspiring more joy, happiness, fulfillment, and success to anyone ready for a change in the status quo. I will make available to the reader practical, easy-to-implement tools, strategies, exercises, and activities that I have successfully used with coaches and athletes in championship cultures for a more caring and connected environment.

For example, to implement the value of selflessness, I tell a story about a professional athlete who gave up his starting role, because it was in the best interest of his team. Then, I offer this exercise for all athletes to use: Every Monday, group text your team telling them what specifically you will do that will demonstrate a "giving attitude," a selfless act of kindness. In this way, they take ownership and accept responsibility with a willingness to be held accountable. We discuss this together and make sure all are on the same page in order to Win the Day.

I also combine this wisdom and experience from my work over the past 30 years with the expertise of twelve nationally acclaimed Hall of Fame head coaches from the professional and collegiate ranks who utilize the core values presented in this book with their championship cultures. Together, they have amassed well over 100 national championships in a variety of sports. I have had the honor of working intimately with most of these iconic coaches and their teams as well as having had the opportunity to talk with and/or simply observe the others.

A point that should not be lost is that these 12 coach examples I've chosen to feature present an interesting mix of personalities, who have used a variety of practices throughout their careers. Despite their disparate approaches and differences in personality, all of them recognized the significance of team culture and were open to learning about how to create environments that allowed themselves and their athletes to excel. There are other, current successful coaches I'm less familiar with to whom I refer to in this book who have cultivated and sustained winning cultures, such as Dabo Swinney, head football coach of the National Championship team—Clemson University.

The following is a list of 12 Hall of Fame coaches, the programs they coached, and the number of national and conference championships they've won as either a coach or an athlete:

COACH	CULTURE	CHAMPIONSHIPS WON
STEVE KERR	Golden State Warriors Basketball	Eight (8)
CINDY TIMCHAL	University of Maryland and USNA Lacrosse	Twenty-one (21)
ANSON DORRANCE	University of North Carolina Soccer	Twenty-two (22)
PHIL JACKSON	Chicago Bulls and L.A. Lakers Basketball	Thirteen (13)
MISSY MEHARG	University of Maryland Field Hockey	Thirty (30)
JOHN WOODEN	UCLA Basketball	Ten (10)
NANCY STEVENS	University of Connecticut Field Hockey	Three (3)
DEAN SMITH	University of North Carolina Basketball	Two (2)
BILL WALSH	San Francisco 49ers Football	Five (5)
BOB HANSEN	Middlebury College and UCSC Tennis	Fifteen (15)
MISSY FOOTE	Middlebury College Lacrosse	Four (4)
PETE CARROLL	Seattle Seahawks and USC Football	Three (3.)

This book applies the expertise and wisdom of these Hall of Fame coaches, through their personal stories, anecdotes, and opinions about crafting their championship cultures. These renowned coaches show how using these core values drives and sustains winning in sports and life. Their contributions appear throughout the book. I also enter the discussion and take on the "heavy lifting," showing how I have implemented these special values and constructed strong, effective, successful team cultures. I also refer to less well-known coaches to comment within the text on their cultural philosophies and how they implement their core values in order to Win the Day.

These core values, emblematic of various championship cultures, include joy, selflessness, competition, mindfulness, gratefulness, integrity compassion, humility, respect, trust, fearlessness, perseverance, love, and many more (see TOC). These essential values, craved and cherished by all coaches and athletes, are imperative in establishing emotionally safe, healthy, and functional environments that promote loyalty, mental toughness, self-esteem, and an eagerness to "go the distance" on or off the court. Such a rigorous inner journey demands an outside-the-box mentality as we gain a sense of higher purpose, something that is bigger than the game itself, our capacity to care more deeply and connect.

These coaches have each built something special with their teams. This book will offer them a broader opportunity to build something special for all of us connected to athletics. The contribution of these coaches to this project becomes a gift for future generations of athletes, coaches, and leaders, seeking guidance on creating healthy cultures and lives. It affords them an additional opportunity to be proactive in changing the status quo by offering their core values to those of us who crave a shift in how we perceive sports as an opportunity for full human capacity. Two of my heroes, Martin Luther King, Jr., and Nelson Mandela, used many of these same values to advocate for positive change, as well as elevating one's performance. I do something similar in this book by using sports as the vehicle to achieve such important, profound, and penetrating change personally and athletically.

Win the Day is a call for change. It is written to help coaches and athletes to know "what's important now?" to connect, to care for each other, and to create, cultivate, drive and sustain a team culture of champions. I do this by using methods, strategies, and core values that empower and guide others to succeed, perform well, and be fearless in emotionally safe, cohesive, loving environments that will help all involved to thrive and be victorious on and off the field. You can't control winning a game, but you can control doing what's important now and Win the Day. When you do, you position yourself for great things to happen.

PART I

CONNECTING AS FAMILY—
Win the Day Culture

I'm convinced that the concept of team connection and family in a culture is right on the money. The relationship piece for coaches is wonderfully profound.

—Anson Dorrance, Head Women's Soccer Coach, UNC

I believe that we are all inextricably connected to each other in a very deep, profound, and spiritual way solidified in love and compassion. Chip Conley, author of *Wisdom @ Work*, affirms my belief as he describes connection as "the empathic capacity to resonate with others ... the capacity for empathy and intimacy." There is no place for the notion of separateness in my cultures. Our so-called "separateness" is an illusion that must be examined and transcended. Author and American philosopher, William James, addresses this illusion, when he claimed: "we are like islands in the sea, separate on the surface but connected in the deep."

The championship cultures I advocate must first learn that we're all connected and find ways to discard the illusion of separateness. We are all human beings not human doings. We all suffer pain, loss, disappointment; we all experience joy, victory, and happiness. My mission is to "Win the Day" and do this in a culture that learns how to break down the barriers and connect for something bigger than us or the game itself.

Win the Day cultures are very much like a flock of Canada geese, migrating to warmer climates; they fly and connect together in a V formation, selflessly giving to each other on this challenging journey. When they connect in this way, they can fly 70 percent further than if they had not done so. Notice how these majestic birds are continually communicating with each other the sweet sounds of encouragement and positive chatter. They could be saying, "way to go big bird, keep it up, looking strong, you can do it."

Win the Day organizations and teams mimic their fine-feathered friends in this way. Organizational management consultant and prolific author, Meg Wheatley, knows

Delmas Lehman/Shutterstock.com

Win the Day cultures are very much like a flock of Canada geese, migrating to warmer climates; they fly and connect together in a V formation, selflessly giving to each other on this challenging journey.

much about the power of team connection. In her insightful book, *A Simpler Way*, she mentions her "organization could accomplish so much more, if they relied on the passion evoked when we connect to others ... so many of us hunger to discover who we might become together."

The wisdom of *The Art of War*, the ancient Chinese book of strategy by Sun-Tzu, reinforces Wheatley's astute observation. In it, Sun-Tzu tells us that a cohesive, unified team, well-connected and competing with one heart and soul, often will defeat a more talented group that lacks such qualities. From my experience with championship teams in various sports, there's nothing more satisfying and astounding than experiencing such a team of inspired, cohesive, well-connected for athletes competing together.

The Art of War is perhaps more relevant for athletes and leadership today than when it was written over 2,000 years ago. He believed that the key to triumph in battle is unity of purpose and connection. In his book, he states:

> *Those who establish a viable group will win, even if they are small. The key to all operations is harmony and connection with people.*

Of course, the "win" he refers to could relate to the acronym WIN, as in "what's important now?" and, more likely, what is important now is how we Win the Day by being connected with our teams, staff, and the game itself.

Strong team cultures are well aware of how synergy and cooperative action impact success. It is the key to team effectiveness in any arena of life. In his insightful book *Playing for Keeps*, David Halberstam talks about how, at the University of North Carolina, under the guidance of iconic coach Dean Smith, "everything was built around the concept of team … In the long run, he believed that you went further by working as a team and sacrificing individually to team effort … it would serve his players better later in their lives." Who could argue with such a successful program—and the success of its graduates 20 years later?

Coach Phil Jackson believes that good teams become great ones when they adopt the notion of selflessness, trust each other, and get beyond the "me" for the "we." He believes that the critical ingredient for a championship is love and connection, the elements of sharing, giving, and deep caring. He recently told me that as an NBA coach, the standard for connection he used was the Native American culture that acknowledged the need to honor opponents, tribe, nature, and life. It is all about connection and compassion, which is how we can Win the Day.

Connection for Coach Pete Carroll's Seattle Seahawks culture is enhanced when we're all being authentic and genuine. This scenario is when strong bonds and relationships happen. He spends a good amount of time on this aspect of team, one of the reasons for much of the success of teams coached by Carroll.

Connection for the Seahawks, as it is with Steve Kerr's Warriors, goes beyond the Xs and Os. These teams create environments in which trust is established, and the relationship game is won. I will get more specific about how to achieve such an environment, as we progress in this book, learning how to implement particular ways to establish such a culture. For now, simply assume that your team is hungry for and craves something in life where your players can be part of a group bigger than themselves and the game itself, doing something for the greater good. In that regard, Anson Dorrance, women's soccer coach at the University of North Carolina, recently told me that he's convinced that this idea about connection in the Win the Day culture is, in his words, "right on the money."

Once again, Meg Wheatley strongly affirms what we've been expressing about the importance and value of connection, when working with teams and organizations. She states that if, "*we took the time to ground our work in the deep connections that engage us, we would be overwhelmed by the energy and contribution so willingly given.*"

The rest of this section of the book will help you discover ways and methods that will facilitate connection within your Win the Day culture.

CULTURAL WISDOM

Culture is what we believe, how we behave, and the experiences that our behavior produces.

—Urban Meyer, Former Head Football Coach, The Ohio State University

Arguably, the biggest buzz in the arena of athletics today is the word culture. My business could exist by working exclusively with teams that wish to build and sustain a healthy, functional team culture. Simply stated, culture is the essential absolute in the success of all teams in sports and life.

On a more poetic level, Daniel James Brown, author of the bestselling book, *Boys in the Boat*, beautifully and clearly describes the spirit of culture: "You become part of something bigger, larger than yourself; you find something you did not know you possessed. There are mystical moments of pride, elation and love for each other. Moments you'll tell your grandchildren. Moments that bring you closer to your maker, forming bonds of trust and affection, a place where all become one. It's a rare thing, it's sacred. It's exquisite, a sense of exhilaration … why we play."

In this passage, Browne reinforces what I've been teaching for years about connection, about interaction, about everyone from top to bottom, working together and engaging in elevating the group imperative. It's what really matters in the building of a champion culture. Continuing along this path, Brown talks about giving of yourself spiritually and emotionally and leaving a piece of your heart to the process. It is comparable to a symphony.

If one is out of tune, the whole group collapses. This situation is no different for any team that desires to experience success. This is what I call *cultural wisdom*.

Culture is a group's identity, the foundation of all championship-level teams. For a coach, culture is a vision put into action. It is a set of clearly defined core values and behaviors that help you Win the Day, as well as drive and sustain winning on the scoreboard and in life. The Latin word for culture is *cultus*, which means to care, requiring nothing less than giving a piece of your heart to others. It's a shared mission of caring and connection, impacting coaches, athletes, and all those individuals connected to the group. It has been said that the success of the US Navy Seals culture is directly related to connection, caring, selflessness, and a pervasive sense of family.

The Japanese have a special word for what I've been referring to as cultural wisdom. It is called *Kaizen*. Conceived of as a way for the country to restore itself after the devastation of WWII, they created a culture similar to the Win the Day philosophy. It was a culture of continual growth and improvement, where all workers at all levels engaged in building a cohesive team together.

Similar to the concept of cultural wisdom, Kaizen sought to humanize the workplace, and create a safe environment where mistakes were instantly corrected; one that would nurture the people and build strong relationships by praise and encouragement, in which everyone felt relevant, important and valued. Kaizen is a Win the Day philosophy, what can be called an action plan—or a mission that takes one day at a time and controls what you can as a way to move slowly and methodically forward to create amazing results in the long-term on a continual basis.

Brasil Creativo/Shutterstock.com

Kaizen, the Japanese word for continuous improvement, entails a culture of continual growth and improvement, where all workers at all levels engaged in building a cohesive team together.

Like Kaizen, Win the Day is the mission keeping all of us on track moving toward future goals of growth, improvement, and ultimate victory. I know that coaches people respect, like Bill Walsh, Pete Carroll, Steve Kerr, Brad Stevens, and Anson Dorrance, are very much aligned with this fascinating concept of Kaizen and see its relationship to winning the day. Their focus is on continuous, steady improvement, in the moment, one day at a time. For example, 49'ers coach Bill Walsh once said, "I have no grandiose plan for winning a championship, but rather a standard and plan for installing a level of competency at which our production level would become higher … on and off the field, than that of our opponents. I had faith the score would take care of itself."

This iconic football coach won five Super Bowls with the San Francisco 49ers. He knows a few things about culture. According to Walsh, "the development of a successful team begins with a successful culture. The culture precedes positive results. It doesn't get tacked on as an afterthought." He called his culture the "standard of performance," which represented the team's core values and ideals, based on high standards, hard work, and strong commitment and connection to all those within the culture.

Years ago, I was honored to have a conversation with Coach Walsh about this, while I was working at Stanford. His comments about culture influenced and changed my approach to teamwork immediately. From that meeting, I began to understand the relevance of culture and core values. It shifted my focus forever, and this book is the summation of all I've learned since that fortuitous moment.

Anson Dorrance, head women's soccer coach at the University of North Carolina, told me he attributes his 22 national championships to the team's 11 core values. "These principles produce our extraordinary results; we do this by how we Win the Day, our practice process." It is based on connection and authentic caring.

University of Alabama head football coach, Nick Saban, believes that you must have a vision of what kind of program you want to have, followed by a plan to implement it, and then develop congruent core values that reflect such a vision.

My friend and role model for much of my leadership and coaching work is Phil Jackson, winner of 13 World Championships in the NBA as both a coach and a player. Jackson compares a championship culture to a tribe of warriors—a unified cohesive group with a strong core of values and a sacred quest, the drive for a championship by winning the day. Unlike a team that simply works together for a common goal, a tribe is a deeply connected group who care about each other's success and buy in to a set of core values that drive winning.

What connects a team is what they do. What connects a tribe is why they do it: for the love of each other and something bigger than winning on the scoreboard. In a recent communication with Phil, he emphasized to me the importance and value of a strong culture, mentioning how "compassion for opponents" is a vital component in a tribe culture. Phil's connection to "tribe" runs deep, having had many years among what he calls "the First American's" culture, the Lakota Nation.

Throughout this book, I will be referencing several points of cultural wisdom to this Lakota Nation, through the profound voice of Joseph Marshall III, a gifted historian, a storyteller, an author of 13 books, and a member of the Sicunga Lakota Sioux. His book, *The Lakota Way*, is filled with relevant values that compare to those I use in my work with teams. In his book, he talks about the concept of cultural wisdom, which ties into Jackson's notion of tribe and the *Win the Day* philosophy. Wisdom, according to Marshall, "comes from the light as well as from the darkness; it gives depth of insight, the perception that only comes from experiencing our numerous struggles." This conceptual premise is exactly connected to the culture wisdom promoted in *Win the Day*.

Over the past 30 years, I have had the honor of being an intimate part of 115 championship teams that drove for and sustained success. For me, the road was rocky, at times, with moments of doubt, but I never lost confidence in the teaching and implementation of those solid standards that I believed would create and sustain a great team, an extraordinary organization regardless of the scoreboard. These were teams where standards were high, and fear was low.

Whether you know it or not, you have a team culture. Not being aware of this reality is to run the risk of leaving its proper development to chance. Notice what works and what doesn't. As coach Steve Kerr noted in the foreword, ask yourself what you value most. What are the overt important values to you, personally, in your life? Narrow them down to the best four that represent you as a human being. What matters to you as a person? Then, help your team to live these values each day. (See section on Core Values.)

Your success depends on your observation of these inner values. Sustained success is intentional and begins with walking the talk. Connecting, setting standards, boundaries, values, and direction help the athletes to be aligned—on the same page. Teams that Win the Day do so by connection, caring and executing their core values. When this situation happens, morale is high, commitment is strong, behaviors are congruent, integrity is demonstrated, goals are more easily attainable, connection is palpable, work ethic is solid, loyalty is apparent, and enthusiasm, excitement, caring, and inspiration are experienced.

When a culture is solid and safe, everyone wins the day. When you Win the Day, adhering to the cultural champion process not only dictates the way you live and compete, it also positions everyone for positive outcomes and results. The essence of a good culture is in how it demonstrates connection, which drives and sustains success. It is a daily process and controllable. It is the standard by which we set the tone that helps to Win the Day. It is the driving force that embodies a sense of toughness, courage, passion, and attitude that helps individuals rise above obstacles when they appear.

Whether winning a championship or not, every team that adopted the core values that I taught, as well as those they chose and developed, lived, played, practiced, and competed like champions. This factor is the essence of *Win the Day*. It was their culture; it was how they—the coaches, athletes, and everyone involved with the program from top to bottom—did things together and connected to each other that led them to believing they could do and be something other than ordinary ... and they did, and they were. In a phrase, the connection in their culture enabled them to Win the Day.

It can be helpful to summarize the aforementioned and consider a vision of what *cultural wisdom* is—a vision that sets a tone and guides you and your team in the culture-building process at all levels of performance, from high school up to the professional ranks. What I suggest you do in implementing these ideas is to sit in your team in a circle and have a full participatory discussion about each one and why it's relevant to your program, answering questions where appropriate:

- Culture is who we are and how we do things "around here." How do we do things around here?
- Culture is about socially transmitted behavior patterns, beliefs, thoughts; these are the traits of the "culture of champs." What are our patterns, beliefs, and traits?

- Culture is a set of predominant attitudes/behaviors that characterize the team. What are ours in this culture?
- A culture is an atmosphere and environment that is welcoming and nurturing. How is this factor true for us?

dsy88/Shutterstock.com

A culture is an atmosphere and environment that is welcoming and nurturing.

- Culturc works togcthcr to arrivc at a common understanding that benefits all members of the team, rather than one person. What does this mean to you?
- Culture is a bond. While it is not essential for everyone to be "best friends" (although this situation is often the outcome), it is crucial to accept and respect other's interests, strengths, and weaknesses. How do we do this?
- Culture is a group that resembles a family. What is a family? How does it act?

- Leadership in a culture that is healthy is everyone's job. Leading is when you reflect the culture you create. What does this proposition mean to us?
- Ritual—all healthy cultures create ritual, be it pre-game, practice, meditation, or visualization, post-game. What is yours? What are ours? Come up with one, if none already exist.

From this point, we can now segue into a deeper understanding of what it means to Win the Day, given our understanding of *cultural wisdom*.

WIN THE GAME OR WIN THE DAY

Through our conversation, emails, and texts, Jerry Lynch helped me to pass on his Win the Day philosophy to our Warrior culture to achieve success. I believe a team culture has to be connective, caring, and authentic and Win the Day. In his book, he'll help you to implement its guiding principles.

—Steve Kerr, Head Coach,
Golden State Warriors

The ancient Chinese book of strategy, *The Art of War* by Sun-Tzu, teaches us that the war is won before the battle begins. In other words, for sports, it's all about preparation, doing all the controllable little things that position us for ultimate victory. It is in reading this 2,000-year-old tome that I first conceived of the Win the Day approach.

When a team shows up to win the game, their focus is on outcomes and results, something they cannot control. In turn, this situation could cause them to become tight, tense, tentative, nervous, fearful, and stressed. When such feelings occur, confidence declines, and self-doubt rises. Losing confidence positions you to compete at levels lower than what's possible, resulting in a lackluster performance.

Conversely, when a team shows up to Win the Day, they focus on all the little things that they can control. For example, a basketball team would concentrate on boxing out, crashing the boards, sprinting the lanes, diving for the 50/50 ball, and playing "in-your-face" defense.

What are the little things in your sports? Ask your athletes to create a list and, when appropriate, do it by position. When you execute your controllables, you become calm, relaxed, and poised. As a result, confidence climbs as self-doubt wanes.

Even the pros, like the Golden State Warriors, forget about their culture norm of winning the day and must be reminded by their coach to show up to simply compete and let the outcome take care of itself. This scenario happened during the Warrior's 2015 championship run, when they were down to the Cleveland Cavaliers in the finals two games to one. The distracting media talked about the fourth "must-win" game. Steve reminded his guys to play Warrior ball, focusing on all the controllable little things and compete in this way. They won big that night on the road to the NBA title, their first of three in four years. As such, they accomplished their goal by winning the day.

I used the concept of Win the Day recently on a visit with one of my teams, the men's tennis squad at Middlebury College. To give a little history, they had played for the national championship the year before and lost in the finals. The team came back determined to win it this past season.

I listened, observed, and noticed how stressed they seemed, even though they hadn't even begun their season, which was four months away from the tournament. They wanted to talk about winning it all, and I suggested that they let that thought go and focus on what's important now? (WIN). I mentioned that when they focus on outcome and results, it's something they can't control, and it can make them tight and tense, which is no way to play tennis.

In its place, I recommended that they focus simply on the important process of being connected with their values and friends, and thereby Win the Day, by doing their mental and physical routines; working hard at a consistent high level, one ball at a time; demonstrating positive body language; supporting each other; being selfless and fearless; demonstrating courage, patience, and perseverance; getting proper rest; eating well; and doing all of this each day. Subsequently, the men's tennis team at Middlebury College adapted the concept, placed the mantra "Win the Day" on the back of a shirt, and rode this focus to winning the national championship.

Their head coach, Bob Hansen, talks about it this way: "Win the Day is a concept that has helped me crystallize what I've been trying to do for years. The guys could get their heads and hearts around this idea and focus on what's most important in the moment. Now, every single practice is a Win the Day event."

Cindy Timchal, coach of a national championship team in women's lacrosse, continues to ride the Win the Day mantra to victory at NAVY. "We shout it out all the time. It helps us to play free, be confident, and release ourselves from competing. It diminishes the fear, because we can believe that winning the day is within our power."

While this Win the Day concept does not guarantee victory on the scoreboard, it does assure that you'll give your all and get the most out of yourself. It helps a team to connect. It is manageable, measurable, and controllable. The following is an inspirational and empowering story about a high school girls' soccer team that learned how to Win the Day from their coach, Sean Stedeford, who was being trained by me during the season. He sent me this very much appreciated email:

I am so excited to tell you about our latest game! The result speaks volumes about our group; but it is not the result that inspired me.

Last Friday, we were sent to play Grandview HS. This is a true David-versus-Goliath matchup. To paint the picture for you, Grandview has 3,200 students, they are currently ranked #7 in the nation, are ranked #1 in 5A "big schools," have been undefeated this season, and were the highest ranked team in all classifications in Colorado. Colorado Academy has 400 students, are currently ranked #2 in 3A, and are not nationally ranked. The day before, we told our team that they were going to have to fight for everything in the game. They had to be disciplined, committed, and accountable to one another. We knew our "soccer" was good enough, but it was our athleticism that was our disadvantage. Grandview were bigger, stronger, faster, etc. … I am willing to bet the majority of folks thought we would lose 7-1. When the whistle blew, none of it mattered!

I have never seen my group play like they did. There was purpose to everything they did. They showed caring and stayed connected. How they passed, how they communicated, how they tackled, and the most impressive thing we saw was *how they played for one another*. They were committed to being connected and a good teammate for the person to their left, right, and behind! For the first time this season, the girls all felt what it was like to pull in the same direction, and as the game went on, their confidence began to soar! Grandview got a goal with three minutes left in the first half, but it didn't matter. The girls were excited at halftime and motivated to get back out on the field. We eventually tied the game at 1-1 off of a corner kick, and you could feel the momentum begin to change. While Grandview was getting frustrated and angry, our girls continued to grow and fight. Soon, we were on the front foot and had opportunities to go ahead in the game. The second half ended 1-1.

Into overtime we went. At this point, we were at 1-1 with the #7 team in the nation! Tiny little CA was showing the soccer world what we are about! Our team culture and family mentality were on full display. In the dying moments of the game, it appeared we were about to give the game away, and our goalkeeper made one of the most spectacular saves I've ever seen to keep Grandview out of the goal. The second overtime ended 1-1, and our girls stormed the field like they had just won the state championship. It meant so much to them. I can't put it into words! They played like warriors. What a moment! We definitely "won the day." We saw a championship caliber team on the field and on the bench. Everyone contributed.

The underlying beauty of this inspirational story is how I've been able to follow this team into the very next season. The story is picked up prior to the last game before the state championship. Sean wrote the following to me:

> I write to you tonight with tremendous excitement! We are headed to the 3A State Championship on Tuesday night. The girls had to battle against tough and resilient teams throughout the playoffs and have earned the opportunity to play for a championship. I am so proud of them!!
>
> We will be playing Jefferson Academy, the only team to beat us this season. They are well organized and athletic, and I know my girls will be looking forward to the challenge. As we approach this penultimate moment in our season, I want to help them focus on creating a moment/memory of every lasting value and not the trophy. Winning a state championship is hard, it's grueling at times, and it can be incredibly emotional. But, it can be a moment in their lives that will and can live forever. When these girls get together at weddings and class reunions, or when they have their own kids, this night is something they will remember. This night is something they will talk about. How can I help them remember it for the right reasons? What advice would you give to focus our attention on Winning the Day?

> They will feel pressure; but this kind of pressure can be used in a positive way, if we can frame it correctly. I am so grateful for this opportunity as a coach, and I feel incredibly blessed to get the pre-championship butterflies once again. Having been here before, you never know when you will be back! I know our tough schedule has prepared us for this moment. Playing the bigger schools, beating nationally ranked programs, and accomplishing so much that has never been done before has been invigorating this season. This is a special group.
>
> Thank you again for all you do and help me with as a coach. Your influence on me has been instrumental in how I communicate and coach this team. When we initially talked in the fall, you told me you had a feeling this would be some of my best work as a coach, and I can confidently say it has.

Subsequently, I then get back with Sean and reassure him about the state championship game:

> Sean…the work has been done. The war is won, before the battle begins. It's because you prepared well, you know what can only be controlled, and you can expect good things to happen because of all this. NOW, tell them this: "I'm not interested in the outcome…I'm interested in how you will be out on the pitch. Be brave, be tough, be the hardest working team on the field and

> NEVER, NEVER GIVE UP, regardless of score." Then, mention in passing, "it's not the size of the dog in the fight; it's the size of the fight in the dog."
>
> And remember...your team will be watching you. Make sure they see your confidence, joy, and calm certainty, even if you must fake it. And have fun as you implement your Divine plan. This is all you can do. All else has been done.

Two days later, I wake up to this joyous email from Sean, after his team has won the Colorado 3A Championship in girls' soccer:

> What a night! Everything we hold close to our hearts in our program was on display last night. I have never been more proud to be the head coach of this program than I was last night. From the outpouring of motivational texts from the alumni, well wishes from other coaches in the state, and watching the girls "compete with their hair on fire" as you say, was just incredible. Words cannot describe the pride I feel today. I wanted to help create a moment of everlasting value in the lives of these girls, and I believe, as they begin to reflect on this season, they will see we created more than simply "one" moment. It was a season to remember. I am sad to see it end, but this group will forever have a place in my heart!

Thank you again for all of your help, guidance, and support! It means the world to me to have someone like you to lean on and learn from as a coach. I have attached my favorite photo from last night. Those smiles make it all worth it!

Yes, they do Sean. I couldn't help myself but to respond to this awesome journey over a two-year period of time:

Hey Sean, I want to congratulate you and your awesome young warriors for your penultimate victory last night. This was more than a win on the pitch, the state championship represents two years of dedication to becoming an extraordinary champion coach who has created a cultural environment where these kids can feel safe and connected and cared for to take the necessary risks to discover their greatness and open up to their full human capacity, without the fear of failure.

> You and your team took the Way of Champions message to heart and followed the *WIN THE DAY* mission KNOWING that there is NO path to a championship… being a champion IS THE PATH. Thanks for the opportunity to work with you and influence your growth and development as a Way of Champions coach.
>
> Much love and chi as you celebrate a victory for living the life of a champion.

He got back after this with this touching, heartfelt reply: "The Win the Day mission has changed not just my coaching, but also my way of viewing my life, and the kids will carry these messages into adulthood."

Implementation

As Steve Kerr noted in his opening quote to this section, at this point, I will help you to implement the principles of how you and your team can begin to Win the Day. I'll remind you that every one of the 115 championship teams with which I've been associated had total "buy-in" to this dynamic process on their path of success.

When I'm asked to help build a championship culture, there are two agreements that must be established up-front. First, the process is not a "fix-it" job, but rather a positive, forward-building creation of a culture. Second, the process is an ongoing, never-ending journey of continual development of a highly functional group, clan, team, tribe, family.

As such, all worthwhile things take time. It could take from two to four years for the transition to occur.

A change, however, is felt immediately. Results of intervention are palpable. Resistance is often felt but that melts away, when the benefits of winning the day take hold, such as feeling valued, important, respected, being cooperative, connected, and selfless.

Right at the outset, you and your team must determine the GOAL for the season. This factor covers a range from being league contenders, to winning more games than last season, to winning the national championship … or accomplishing any goal that will be satisfying and feel successful, if achieved. Yes, these are usually outcome goals and serve as guides along the path to keep everyone on track. Think of a lighthouse in the distance that helps direct you to your desired destination. Goals are items that are challenging and attainable, yet not controllable.

Next, we leave that goal for now and focus on a MISSION, a factor that is both challenging and attainable, yet can be controlled. The mission is a day-to-day process-oriented objective that, when executed consistently, keeps you constantly moving toward your GOAL. For my cultures, that mission is always the same, regardless of the goal, i.e., Win the Day, every day in all aspects of your life. I tell them: IT'S A CHOICE! You can do it!

To show up and Win the Day, I suggest that the team (the coaches and the athletes) sit in their circle (see next section on Sacred Circle) and develop a list of PROMISES that are a reflection of the culture, as well as detail specific strategies that help you "compete like crazy, with your hair on fire." The teams with which I work actually use this affirmation to keep on task with their mission.

I emphasize the importance of promising to adhere to the rules of our cultures. When a team buys-in, the result is beautiful, a work of art. The most recent example of going along with this notion of promises was the 2017 women's lacrosse team at the US Naval Academy. Unranked in the top 20 nationally, they managed to stay connected and make it all the way to the final four, only to be defeated by one goal in the semifinals. On the way there, they beat three top 10 teams in the tournament, including a stellar victory over #2 North Carolina on the Tarheels' home field.

According to their Hall of Fame coach, Cindy Timchal, the midshipmen were able to accomplish this enormous feat, because the athletes strongly stayed connected, showed up, and promised to Win the Day every day. Cindy and I had them make these promises, which we referred to as "never-never land."

- Never give up, never, regardless of the score, the crowd, the opponent.
- Never lose confidence by focusing on outcomes. Focus, instead, on the controllables, which give you confidence.
- Never let an opponent defeat your spirit, identity, or culture.
- Never be afraid of errors, mistakes, losing. They're our greatest teachers.
- Never try to go BIG … just execute all the little things over and over.
- Never fail to respond immediately after a mistake—instant positive response.
- Never whine or create drama unnecessarily.

The USNA women's lacrosse team continued to Win the Day by being the toughest, hardest working, tenacious, fearless team on the planet. They competed like crazy, with their hair on fire.

PROMISES, such as those in a Win the Day culture, are written down and discussed frequently. They are meant to be kept. As such, they become convenient, pertinent, specific coaching points during practices and games. You can even have the athletes write on a large index card (which can be laminated) the following: I (fill in the name), promise to uphold with great integrity, the following promises that define who we are, why we compete, and what our cultural identity is all about, and then sign the statement as a signal of commitment. The following are examples of some other non-technical, character promises I have used with teams over the years. Ask your team to identify theirs and/or use the following:

I PROMISE TO:

- Be selfless and give to my team for a cause bigger than any one of us.
- Respond instantly, after I make a mistake.
- Be the hardest worker I can be.
- Be a positive influence on my team and coaching staff.
- Help my teammates feel valued, important, relevant, and respected.
- Give one positive comment to one person, one day at a time.
- Compete with and challenge my teammates in practice, because I love them.
- Respect my opponent, the fans, the officials, and the game.

The following is a list of promises I collected from the Boulder High School boys' soccer team, which has won two state championships and is currently ranked number one this year, using these as a way for them to Win the Day. Their culture is called La Familia, the family. Personally, I love their reference to an imaginary "multiverse."

- This season, we are the most academically eligible student-athletes in the multiverse.
- This season, we are the most focused student-athletes in the multiverse.
- This season, we are the hardest working student-athletes in the multiverse.
- This season, we have the most chemistry of any team in the multiverse.
- This season, we respect each other, the opponent, the program and our school.
- This season, we have more love for each other than any team in the multiverse.
- This season, we are the happiest team in the multiverse.
- This season, we are the most prepared of any team in the multiverse.
- This season, we are the most persistent of any team in the multiverse.
- This season, we have the most dedicated of any team in the multiverse.
- This season, we are selfless to each other and our program, more than any team in the multiverse.

Aside from these profound promises, we can also choose to Win the Day by executing what we can control tactically. Teams can promise to do certain things from a technical standpoint. I help teams to decide what those items may be. They differ, depending upon the sport and position a player holds on that team.

Once again, the circle is used as a sacred signal and symbol to begin this exercise. The first step is to divide the team into smaller circles, when appropriate (individual sports need no division) making the groups by position. Next, each group is asked to identify specific, crucial, relevant, technical strategies and tasks that are controllable, such as diving for the 50/50 ball in basketball. Each group is encouraged to identify 5-10 items. Then, the groups come back into the main circle and openly discuss the points on their list to make sure nothing of importance has been left out. While coaches can really give valuable input in this instance, they should first let the team do the "heavy lifting," because when the players identify something, it comes from them. As such, their commitment and buy-in are stronger.

Once lists are formed, they become a natural extension of the *promises* to keep. I then ask the teams to combine all of their wisdom arrived at together with our cultural norms, collectively as identity that no one, at any time, can prevent us from the choice of executing them wholeheartedly. Later on in this book, the core values of a culture will be addressed. A formula for a successful culture looks like this: character promises + technical promises + core values = Win the Day, competitive champion culture. Furthermore, it's all a CHOICE—items you can control. The execution of these promises and values is called COMPETING. The teams can then affirm: When we compete, we're difficult to beat; we compete like crazy, with our hair on fire.

What if I told you—do all of the aforementioned, and I promise you'll win a championship? How many of you would do it? Well, I can't promise or guarantee you this outcome. On the other hand, I can promise you that if you do all of this, you will experience one of your greatest sports seasons of your life and have more fun than ever before. It is a CHOICE!

At this point, it can be helpful to next segue into the importance and value of our cultural signal and symbol, the sacred circle of a champion culture.

SACRED CIRCLE: SIGNAL AND SYMBOL

In the circle of life, we are all connected. It's designed to create unity. We are all equal in the circle. We are all one, related. The power of the world always works in circles.

—*Oglala Lakota Nation*

Every one of the 115 championship cultures with whom I have worked Win the Day by connecting in a circle. This gesture aligns them with our core values, our mission, our goals, and our "WHY" … why we come together and play the game. Not only is it a signal for everyone to connect, it also announces that we are ready to begin our work. It's a signal to remind us that we are here for each other to Win the Day and begin the work we promised to complete.

The circle has been used also as a sacred symbol for thousands of years by various ancient cultures, such as Celtic, Taoist, Buddhist, and Native American traditions. For the American Indian, the circle is the symbol of Mother Earth in complete balance, with no beginning and no end. They have referred to it as the "Sacred Hoop." Chief Black Elk, Lakota warrior and visionary, reminds us how all of the power of the world forms the shape of a circle. The Lakota nation gathered in circular formations, because the circle was a symbol of connection and harmony in their universe.

I believe that this sacred symbol is perhaps more relevant and profound today than ever. For my work, it is emblematic of the connection, caring, and core values of the cultures I help create with athletic teams. All of my teams use the circle as a reference point and reminder of who we are, what we do, and most importantly, why we do it. The significance of the circle is particularly germane to sports, when you think about it. Almost all balls are round; a home run is referred to as a round tripper—you round the bases; you play a round of golf placing the ball in a round circular hole; basketball is often called a game of hoops or round ball; you circle the bases in baseball; the circle appears in center court and on the midfield line; defenses and offenses mimic circular patterns. In reality, the examples are extensive.

From the very beginning, I introduce my teams to the power of the circle and ask them to conduct their practices and games from that sacred space and go outward from there. When we assemble in the circle for the first time, I quickly remind them of its significance for our culture, as

AustralianCamera/Shutterstock.com

According to the Lakota Indians, all of the power of the world forms the shape of a circle.

well as what I want them to take from it and apply to our team's journey. The following is what I talk about with them, and I encourage you to do the same, when you introduce this cultural iconic symbol to your team. In that regard, you should get your team into a closed circle and say:

- As we stand in this circle, notice how we stand together, side by side, unified as one, connected and cohesive.
- Notice that the circle represents the universal, divine mystical journey with no ending.
- The center of the circle is an empty space. Let it be a reminder of how we keep our minds empty, full of potential, ready to fill it with all that we need to know as we go forward open and receptive to new possibilities. In Japanese, this "negative space" is called Ma, reminding us to step back and see with a whole perspective. It is the concept of less is more.
- The shape of the circle is the letter "O," which stands for our ONENESS of heart, oneness of soul, one mission, one goal. Feel connected with our hearts.
- The shape allows us to see each other, eye to eye, the eyes being the windows to the soul, communicating non-verbally our readiness to serve one another and go to battle for something bigger than each other.
- Notice how we are all equal … no one in front of you, no one in back, no one above you, no one below. We are equal, yet diverse, whole, and inclusive, connected, and strong.
- We are a protected boundary, not to be penetrated by the opponent or unwelcomed.
- With your eyes closed, feel the energy and strength of our group. Remember your promises to go out and Win the Day.

Jacob Lund/Shutterstock.com

The shape of the circle is the letter "O," which stands for our ONENESS of heart, oneness of soul, one mission, one goal.

At first, you may have to read this to the group, until you have memorized it. Either way, the power of the circle is felt by all. Every time the team enters the circle—before the start of practice, prior to a game, and team locker-room meetings, as well as bonding and team building exercises—the athletes can feel such power. I always use the circle as the starting point of any team activity, which signals … we are ready to begin.

Implementation

I also use the circle to create deeper connection, caring, and unity. For example, the following team-bonding exercise uses the circle, which I call the "sharing circle." To begin the exercise, holding a ball or other object of the game, like a stick, bat, or racquet, a person passes it clockwise around the circle. Only those individuals who hold the object can speak. If a person chooses to not talk, the object simply gets passed forward. What's said in the circle remains in the circle. Athletes are directed to share thoughts on important topics—how they feel about the culture, self, opportunity, the benefits of being in the group, etc.—thoughts that are a positive reflection of the awesome culture. Each person who speaks is permitted two to three minutes to do so.

Using the same format, you can run what I call the circle of affirmation. In this exercise, the person holding the object says positive, affirmative statements about how they feel about the next in line as a person, an athlete, and a teammate. Again, speakers are allowed one to two minutes to speak in this exercise. Everyone must speak.

Both of these exercises—you can be creative and make up your own—develop a group imperative, being present and mindful together. It creates a warm, safe place, conducive to building connection. It changes any negativity to positive chi, as you reconnect from the heart, come close in friendships, and are more aware of the power of your influence in the Win the Day culture.

This section is concluded with one of my favorite quotes, pointing to the global relevancy of this sacred symbol of our cultures:

> *Everything an Indian does is in a circle, and that is because the power of the World always works in circles, and everything tried to be round … The sky is round, and I have heard the earth is round like a ball, and so are all the stars. The wind in its greatest power whirls; birds make their nest in circles, for theirs is the same religion as ours. The sun comes forth and goes down again in a circle. The moon does the same, and both are*

round. Even the seasons form a circle in their changing, and always come back again to where they were. Our teepees were round like the nests of birds. And they were always set in a circle, the nation's hoop."

—Chief Black Elk, Medicine Man and Holy Man, Oglala Lakota Indians

THE NEW NORMAL

We purposely move outside our comfort zone, we think outside the box into areas that are unknown and frightening, and this has become our new normal.

—Bob Hansen, Men's Tennis Coach, National Champions, Middlebury College

I love this quote. In reality, much of what I do is outside of the box and my comfort zone, which I like. That's what my brand Way of Champions is all about. Accordingly, as you can see from this book, most of my work is unconventional: I'm not your typical sports psychologist.

In fact, only 15 percent of my work could be called sports psychology. I'm not as interested in fixing problems as much as I am in creating new normal—progressive cultures, based on the 115 championship cultures I've helped to build throughout a long, fun-filled career. I'm interested in profound change—more of the emotional, spiritual type. I weave a quilt of various cultures from Taoist, Buddhist, and Native American cultures, together with Western psychology, in order to Win the Day. I am regarded nationwide as a sports philo-psychological coach, using philosophy and spirituality to construct championship teams in athletics and life. The following are my Win the Day "new normal" strategies to help you and your athletes to stay focused, mindful, and present.

Implementation

❑ Investment Season

Most athletic teams in the sports world have what they call an "off season" … that's normal. My teams, and now yours, do not have such a season. In the spirit of Native American tradition, we have as our new normal, the family "investment season," based on a selfless, giving mode. Working together for something bigger than any one of us. The following is how I implement this season with my teams, using lacrosse as an example. When "fall ball" is over around the middle of November, the athletes typically have approximately two months "off" during the holidays, and when they return, they have lost the big edge they built up with hard work all fall.

What I do for my athletes is invite them to INVEST in their team, so that they can collect dividends down the road. I appeal to them through one of our core values (Selflessness – see Part IV) by asking them to find ways to give, through work, to their teams. It unfolds in the following way:

- How do you specifically want to be physically and mentally when we begin our season in two months?
- What specifically do you need to do to make that happen? Your list can include items like go to the gym, practice stick skills, play wall ball, do cardio workouts, etc.
- Then I say, from your long list, choose four items that you'd be willing to commit to, so you raise your level, come back fit, and do this as a way to GIVE to your team one truly fit teammate, in shape, ready to charge on the first day back. Do this as a way to demonstrate the value of selflessness. Tell the athletes how this is the investment season, their new normal.

- Encourage them to form convenient small groups to keep each other motivated and focused. They can do group texts to keep checking progress.

❑ Heart From the Start

A new normal idea that I know you'll want to implement immediately is called "heart from the start." It's a simple concept, based in mindfulness. How many times have you experienced your team, in practice or a game, come to the field and have a sluggish start? They sit back and wait to see what develops, so they can go with the flow. Before they realize it, they have fallen behind and struggle to get back into the event.

Song_about_summer/Shutterstock.com

"Heart from the start" is a simple concept, based in mindfulness.

Admittedly, there are certain times when it might be a good strategy to go with the flow, but I believe that most of you may be thinking, "I want us to BE THE FLOW." If that is your goal, then your culture can establish your new normal called "heart from the start." Being mindful of this phrase and attaching a specific action plan that describes what this looks like, and what it means specifically to begin the game in this way, you can practice it daily. As a result, when the time comes, the execution is a precise replication of that action plan.

The phrase "heart from the start" becomes the affirmation mantra that will "jump start" your competitive juices, as you compete with your hair on fire. Remember, for this to work well, you must identify specific behaviors or actions you wish to execute and then practice them on a regular basis. Coming out on fire in the first five minutes of a game sends a convincing message to opponents that you mean business.

❑ Instant Positive Response—IPR

Once again, in traditional cultures, the athletes' response to a mistake, a miscue, or an error is to drop their head and shoulders, feeling sorry for themselves and embarrassed, because they believe they let the team down. During the time it takes to grieve the error, the opponent scores in offensive transition or establishes an advantageous position on the field. As a result, two mistakes are made at the same time: the original error, as well as the mistake of not responding properly. Because of the frequency of such an occurrence, I developed the concept of IPR, instant positive response. My teams practice this new normal daily, and when an error occurs, they communicate loudly on the field "IPR, IPR" to get the athlete, who committed the mistake, back into the hurried flow of the next play. Being mindful of this idea actually helps athletes to commit fewer errors. As we know, however, there are two types of athletes—those who make mistakes … and those who will.

❑ Three Talents

If you are creating a Win the Day culture, you and your athletes must agree that there are three talents in your system. The first one is obvious, and most teams you play will have it. It's called PHYSICAL TALENT. You can work with athletes on improving this talent, yet for the most part, maturation and time help to develop this factor if you're a good teacher.

The second talent is MENTAL TALENT or mentality. In reality, not every team is mentally talented. On the other hand, more and more often, to train this aspect of performance, sports psychologists are being hired on all competitive levels of performance, up to and including the pros. You even see this with kids as young as five or six in sports like gymnastics, tennis, and golf. There's a lot of room for development with this talent, and it's growing rapidly.

The third talent is one I call SPIRITUAL TALENT. Very few teams are working on this aspect of performance, and, arguably, it is one of the most important pieces in championship cultures that I help to develop. Few people know how to strengthen this talent. My brand, Way of Champions, specializes in this crucial aspect of championship performance. By spiritual talent, I'm not talking about religion. Rather, it relates to the specific "heart"-directed character traits, such as courage, commitment, patience, perseverance, tenacity, fearlessness, accountability, integrity, vulnerability, and resilience, to name a few.

The good news is these can be learned and, therefore, taught. Furthermore, this is what this book *Win the Day* is all about. You'll find all of these and more in Parts III

PopTika/Shutterstock.com

Spiritual talent relates to the specific "heart"-directed character traits, such as courage, commitment, patience, perseverance, tenacity, fearlessness, accountability, integrity, vulnerability, and resilience, to name a few.

and IV. In fact, as you peruse this book, you will discover many more ways that you can employ to create outside-the-box, unconventional, new normal sports cultures.

❑ Compassionate Warriors

This attribute is the fifth element of the new normal. As you get more familiar with the Win the Day cultural tenets, and the undergirding philosophy and foundation of the Way of Champions brand, I can tell you that they have their roots in the ancient Tibet legendary kingdom of Shambhala, located high in the Himalayas. It was a culture of enlightened warriors, valiant fighters of indomitable spirit. They were considered fearless, tenacious athletes of iron will. They were armed with weapons of the heart, such as courage, integrity, and fortitude. (If not already, this will begin to sound familiar as you read on.) They perceived loss, obstacles, and failure as opportunities to learn, grow, and become more aware. These warriors sacrificed for others, worked hard when no one was looking, remained accountable, and did not need to win to be successful. Opponents were partners. You became comfortable with being uncomfortable. You enjoyed the journey, willing to suffer, sacrifice, and even fail, if that's what it would take.

So, as you might imagine, Warriorship is a rigorous spiritual training that awakens all who take the journey to higher levels of personal performance. It relies on this ancient tradition, while providing a valuable modern application of such training for athletics, fitness, and present-day life. In the words of the Chinese sage Lao Tzu, "Keep the ancient, flow with the present." You need to know that the Warriorship Way is a never-ending journey; mastering it simply means staying on track. This book is meant to help you to do just that, to keep you on this path, to continually Win the Day.

DON'T WORRY, BE HAPPY

In order to be happy in life, you need to have something to do, someone to love, something to believe in, and something to look forward to.

—Lou Holtz, Retired, Hall of Fame Football Coach

The underlying wisdom of this quote is its relevance to great cultures in sports that Win the Day by focusing on these four elements. Happiness is something that can be consistently controlled. It is about taking firm, deliberate, intentional ACTION to mindfully LET GO of those negative, emotional weather patterns that detract from a well-connected, caring, healthy culture. Successful sports cultures have important things to do, nurture love through hard work, believe in themselves, and look forward to the opportunities for growth and expansion. The solid relationships that are developed in champion cultures contribute to happiness.

What I have observed over several decades of teamwork is how all those champion Hall of Fame coaches emphasize joy and happiness throughout their Win the Day cultures. Coach John Wooden taught happiness during his champion run. He would tell his athletes how happiness is being at peace with yourself, knowing that you are making the effort, the full effort to do what is right.

For coaches like Bob Hansen at Middlebury and Cindy Timchal at Navy, joy and happiness are an integral aspect of their multiple championship cultures. Both coaches actively encourage happiness daily by creating fun in the execution of a well-designed practice and game plan. Laughter is a method used to relieve stress and fear, as well as not taking yourself too seriously. In their cultures, there is the joy and happiness of a challenging, hard-working, demanding practice, and they celebrate their efforts at the completion of their diligent efforts. Silly mistakes made by all become an excuse to happily bond, embracing their human tendencies. Cindy actually sent me a text recently telling me that "my happiest athletes are the most productive and being productive reinforces their happiness."

What I notice about champion cultures and athletes is how often they seem happy. Of course, it makes me wonder if they are happy because they are champions, or are they champions because they are happy. I think both scenarios are true, but because happiness is a habit

matimix/Shutterstock.com

The solid relationships that are developed in champion cultures contribute to happiness.

that is controlled by your daily actions, the mindset of a champion, Win the Day athlete and team is one in which their actions create their emotional state. It's a CHOICE they make. It's a characteristic of a champion mentality.

They feel happy day to day, generally, and that helps them to be connected and carries over to their performance. Win or lose, they still tend to be happy. On the other hand, when you are happy, don't you usually perform your best? OK, you may not *always* perform your best, when happy, but to perform *well* you must be happy.

Implementation

In champion team cultures that I've experienced, I actually coach the coaches and their athletes on how to find happiness. I encourage, inspire and empower them to be happy, and by doing so, Win the Day. To accomplish this circumstance, we commit to giving up or letting go of the following emotional vampires, habits that block our path to happiness. Accordingly, you are invited to GIVE UP the following:

- Always having to be right. Ask yourself: would you rather be happy or right?
- Trying to control everything, which will reduce stress and create a more relaxed state of being.
- Blaming and pointing fingers at others, which create unnecessary drama.
- Negative self-talk. Negativity weakens your body and dampens your spirit.
- Complaining or whining, when life doesn't go your way.
- Expectations of others and self-pressure.

- Excuses—be accountable, responsible, and vulnerable.
- Limiting beliefs. Beliefs are limits that can be transcended, when examined.
- Fear of failure, our greatest teacher. Fear weakens you. It's the greatest obstacle to performance.
- Resisting change. Change is constant.

These elements, when changed, will impact everything else during your day in a positive way, as you continue to control what you can to Win the Day. Imagine for a moment, how your life would be, how you'd perform if your culture were filled with others committed to letting go of the aforementioned top 10 roadblocks to happiness. It's a CHOICE! Make it part of your culture's promises and keep each other accountable. Make posters and signs about each of these and display them throughout the athletic facility.

Happiness is healthy for all of us. It can cure illness and extend life and raise the level of performance. It relieves depression, anxiety and stress. It relaxes all of the body's muscles, providing an overall sense of wellness. All of this directly contributes to a solid culture of high performance. Remember that you can create it at any time. Choose to look on the bright side of things and let go of the 10 emotional aforementioned vampires.

There is no way to happiness, happiness is the way.

—Thich Nhat Hanh, Zen Buddhist monk

TEAM CULTURE MAGIC

The strength of the team is each individual member. The strength of each member is the team.

—*Phil Jackson, Retired, Hall of Fame NBA Coach*

The magic of the power of a harmonious group is an important feature that has made *The Art of War* one of the most widely read books among generals, corporate CEOs, and athletic coaches throughout the world. The Chinese book of change, *I Ching*, teaches that the human spirit is nourished by a sense of connectedness and unity. As coach Jackson says in the aforementioned quote, each member is strengthened by a well-connected, cohesive, unified team. When you experience this situation, magic happens.

When I work with teams that demonstrate connectedness and harmony, it is pure magic. I notice something special about them … how they walk, talk, run, play. It's different in a special way. The following passage describes my experience after being with such a team during an action-packed, intense final-four weekend. I gave each member of the team a copy, and I want you to have a sense about their dance, their way, one that mesmerized all who came to watch. I wish we all could experience the magic of such a team:

> *In my view, the athletes who play on this team do so because there is a magic to it, one that is hard to find in life. Partly, this magic resides in the physical sensation and pleasure of catching a*

ball on the run, sprinting to the goal for a score. Part of the magic is in the psychological realm where we feel the trust, security, and confidence from being together all season.

In the spiritual domain, it is the safe, comfortable place created to help us take risks and look foolish or fail, so necessary to discover what we are made of, the juice of life, a way of being, not only on the field, court, arena, but in the larger game of life. There is not only the relationship with team, coach, and self, but our relationship to the stick, the ball … all an extension of our hearts, our souls, an expression of who we are.

There is also an aesthetic component of the team, one that demonstrates the absolutely most beautiful way of playing and competing. Just as

vchal/Shutterstock.com

When I work with teams that demonstrate connectedness and harmony, it is pure magic.

> *ballet is the most beautiful way of moving the body between two points, our team is to your sport, as ballet is to walking. It is the magical ultimate Win the Day experience incorporating body, mind and spirit. So many other teams wish they could dance like you rather than experience, a dance form more rigid, forceful, less fluid, and contrived. These are forms without soul, without heart, without courage.*
>
> *When these teams see you, they discover a more disciplined, beautiful, flowing way, free of fear, filled with compassion, all of which fills the void, the holes in the soul. They crave your dance and are not sure what it is or how you're being. They just know they are tired of being the wallflowers in the big dance. They want a piece of the magic you own, yet, until they let go of the need to fight you, beat you, destroy you and simply play the game or dance the dance, the magic will be forever elusive.*

This team won the national championship, but more importantly, they won the day as well as the hearts of all who came to experience their demonstration of passion and love for each other and for the game. They were being champions even before the outcome was decided. The next year, at the final four, the team t-shirts read: DANCE ON. They did and won, once again.

Magic happens when you remember to remain connected to your love and passion for the game and each other, and become so much more. In what ways is your team culture magical? Notice what happens when you embrace the Win the Day philosophy.

LA FAMILIA CULTURA

We are La Familia and we compete with love, connection, caring, and a strong work ethic. When we do, we Win the Day.

—Hardy Kalisher, Head Coach Boys' Soccer, Boulder (CO) High School

I love the lyrics from the 1960's hit song (sung by Dionne Warwick) "What the world needs now is love, sweet love." I thought about it the moment I read this letter from a coach to his team, the athletes' parents, and the community. Hardy Kalisher, head coach of the Colorado State Champion Boulder High boys' soccer team, sent it to me, knowing about my love for team culture work in sports and life. Hardy's team philosophy is a strong commentary on recapturing ethical, spiritual guidance now, more than ever. La Familia, the family, is the essence of how to make our athletic environment a better place to be through caring and connection. As a culture, they have openly adopted my Win the Day philosophy and use this active mantra prior to practice and each game: Win the Day is How We Play. The following is what Coach Kalisher wrote to me:

Dear Dr. Lynch,

Below is a letter I recently sent to my players and families at the end of our fall season. We were upset, as the defending State Champions, in the second round of the State playoffs, after being ranked #3 in the nation. My goal was to give some perspective and continue to make it a learning and growing experience.

At the end of 80 minutes the effort of the La Familia (Boulder High Soccer's nickname for our team culture) was never questioned. The Boulder High School Boys' Soccer student-athletes had made a promise to each other several months earlier, and they kept that promise. They trusted each other, and they played for each other.

That's been their motivation all season and for the seniors, over the past four years. To play for as long as they can, because this is where they want to be—with each other. It was never about the ring, the ranking, the wins, the rivalries … it was about the journey of becoming young men who have learned how to be fully present in this moment of time. A moment in time. It's about being fully alive in our joy and our pain. We are fortunate to be in the position to experience both.

Fabrizio Andrea Bertani/Shutterstock.com

La Familia, the family, is the essence of how to make our athletic environment a better place to be through caring and connection.

These are essential and important years for teenagers, as they become young men. As coaches and players, we have a great responsibility to each other. As a team with 19 seniors, it truly has been a four-year process of becoming young men. Young men who are ready to model for their friends, peers, and families, how to be men who have earned confidence through integrity, compassion, honesty, empathy, vulnerability, and selfless effort. Young men who have experienced the transformational power of being in a community, based on love and brotherhood.

It takes courage for a teenage boy to step into that arena. It takes courage for anyone. It takes courage to step into that arena and look at your peers and tell them, 'I love you, and I'll give you all I have so that you can thrive! I am committed to our culture and values, and I will transform into the best version of myself … for you.'

That's why La Familia is always a team of overachievers. Because, over their four-year journey, they achieved what they never knew they could.

We didn't win every game. But these Panthers are perfect in every way. They never lost the motivation or connection to WHY we play the WAY we play. It's so much more than soccer.

What is our Why? Our why is La Familia. It's the boys becoming brothers, and brothers becoming the kind of young men you would want your sons and daughters to call friends, colleagues, and family. It's about making our community a better place, so that the world is a better place. It may start with a soccer ball, but our Why continues on, regardless of what goal the ball ends up in.

When the 2017 Panthers left the field last night, it was a sad locker room, maybe the saddest I've seen in 42 years of soccer, and I've lost plenty of big games. Sad not because of the game, but because of the end of the team's season. No more practice. No more locker room. No more runs together over the wooden bridge to Recht Field. But after 90 minutes of sharing stories of joy, admiration, and giving gratitude in the locker room, our locker room, these young men stepped out the door with hearts full of love. Love for each other and gratitude for the journey—their process of becoming the best versions of themselves. There is no there, there in La Familia, because it does not stop. We set the goals, but we celebrate Who we become.

Losing games is as important as winning. The season coming to an end is part of the process. Losing at home in the playoffs hurts that much more, but turning the loss into the seeds of real growth is why these young men are and will always be Champions. This team is not and never was going to be defined by one win or one loss. The legacy of La Familia will continue to grow because of them. The next wave of Panthers is ready.

To see young men, just boys a few months ago, look each other in the eyes and call their teammates their heroes, their role models, and their inspirations gives me belief in our collective future as humanity. Not hope, but honest belief.

The world needs more love, and these young men are ready. To see our youngest student-athletes in the locker room make promises to keep the legacy alive makes me proud that the culture of La Familia will continue. To see my assistant coaching staff share their pride, thanks, and love for the time they have with these young men reminds me, again, that these are the coaches that we want our teenagers to play under. To see the thanks, trust, and love the parents and families give back in support of La Familia makes us proud to be your son's coaches.

To see the support pour in from the community of students, administrators, teachers, coaches, alumni, and others well beyond the school campus reinforces and validates that we have something special here. To see my former players being the coaches and mentors to these teenagers makes me proud.

There is no there, there … we are here. We are La Familia and we play with love, connection, caring, and effort. We focus on how to Win the Day.

—Coach Hardy Kalisher

I include this beautiful statement, because I believe it represents the summation of all that I write about in this book. I was completely in awe, when I read it. A week after I received this heart-felt narrative about his championship culture, we talked on the phone to discuss his work that is having an impact on other athletic programs in the Boulder County area, helping young coaches to create and sustain similar championship cultures. He is being actively recruited to share his cultural core values by speaking with many athletic programs. He is an extraordinary coach who really understands how it's all about winning the relationship game. In our phone conversation, Hardy seemed open, genuine, authentic, and vulnerable—all of the essential traits coaches need to connect and sustain strong relationship with the athletes. In his own words, "I tell them that I love them."

Several months after meeting Hardy, I was able to meet and talk with his team, prior to an important game during their season. It confirmed for me all that the coach had written about in that first email he sent to me. The following is his analysis of that game I witnessed. This assessment gave me a first-hand connection to the team in action, coupled with coach Hardy's profoundly deep work in the development of such a strong culture:

> *Tonight, I was so proud of how the boys worked through the high pressure of the opposing team's effort. We need those challenges. I was especially proud to see young Jesse carry his inspiration from Tuesday night's conversation with the two of us into his pregame locker room talk. He nailed it, when he communicated his interpretation of your insights and wisdom back to his teammates. He asked to talk to them, and I was proud of*

him. And then his great effort and composure resulted in his first three-goal game ever. That doesn't happen for him without his new focus on winning the day. Jesse really stepped up tonight as our "on-the-field leader" when Omar, who typically has that role, was feeling sick.

Only a week ago, we weren't fully confident that Jesse would be a starter on the team! He knew it, and it was a challenge and opportunity that I think we both were committed to work through. I believe Jesse really had a transformational breakthrough in his leadership and spirit, which elevated the way he played. I've seen it in past seasons with other players, and it really is a joy to witness. I thank you for being his spark on Tuesday night. We were both looking for that magic spark moment to happen. And then to see it actualized, as he competed, what a gift! Thank you!

What I was most proud of at the end of the game, and what I told the boys after the game, was how a few boys who usually don't receive very much playing time, brought a tremendous effort to the second half of the game, especially the last 25 minutes and how they helped reinforce the power of our WHY.

One of the things I personally took away from this week, and, I thank you for the lesson, is the reminder to see my team. By that, I mean to really look them in the eyes with love and see each of them one at a time; to thank and acknowledge each of them, as well as my assistant coaches and support staff. This step requires that I be vulnerable enough to allow myself to see each of them as individuals. That effort takes only a few moments and is essential! To have a deeper connection requires that I allow them to see me, which in turn creates a moment where they can see themselves being seen. They see their own humanity. If that makes sense? When they are seen with love, they feel safe and appreciated as "a human being and not as a human doer."

I am fully aware, as coach, that I'm modeling for them how they can see each other as authentic, confident, and compassionate young men—a model that young men need in this day and age. That is the goal. To create a culture where they can truly see each other. That they can be vulnerable and open to exchanging gratitude and love like they exchange passing the ball on the field.

The ball is really a metaphor. The ball is round. It wants to be passed and exchanged amongst the teammates. It's in the ball's nature to be shared. It's the same with the spirit of this soccer program. Pass the love and exchange the spirit and energy. It's actually in our human nature. All we have to do is allow ourselves to be free. That's what creates the spirit of La Familia or what we called tonight in our pregame talk, "the special sparkle in the eyes." And that is real strength and empowerment.

Yes, it takes courage, but courage comes easier, when you feel safe. I am grateful for the honor it is to be with these boys. I know it's only a moment in time, and our time is limited. Thank you for the reminder to be fully present in seeing each of them.

This connection and how the boys feel are all that actually matters. It's my Why. I've coaches and played in enough games and won enough championships to know that they fade into distant memories. But the Why is what really makes me and the layers feel fulfilled. Yes, the wins will take care of themselves, and the losses are great lessons, but it's that love that keeps us all coming back to La Familia.

Coming full circle from the introduction of this book where my "WHY" was addressed in this instance, we have a culture with Hardy set up to make a difference, change the status quo, and, hopefully, convince his athletes to believe that the La Familia culture and their lives can be something other than ordinary.

Oleksandr Osipov/Shutterstock.com

In today's world of sports, coaching, and performance, teams crave a model of diversity, connection, authenticity, and love, using core values that drive and sustain winning.

In today's world of sports, coaching, and performance, teams crave a model of diversity, connection, authenticity, and love, using core values that drive and sustain winning. It's what we need now. In that regard, we need to make proactive change by educating others on how to use the timeless core values put forth in this book, which will provide a strong ethical and spiritual compass for your personal culture. I suggest using La Familia as your guide on this magical journey. When we care and connect using the core values, strategies, tools, and methods discussed and demonstrated in this book, we truly Win the Day.

PART II

LEADING WITH CARE—
Win the Day Coaching

Every member of your team loves to feel wanted and appreciated.

If they are on the team you must find a way to make them feel important and valued.

—Ron Dubois, Head Men's Basketball Coach, UCSC

Part II of our Win the Day journey begins with a recent interview I was honored and privileged to have with iconic head coach Pete Carroll of the NFL champion Seattle Seahawks. Knowing he was a proponent of the Win the Day philosophy of coaching, you can imagine how excited I was to ask him a series of questions that would illuminate the secrets of the Seahawks culture. The meeting was awesome. While he generously answered every question I threw his way with contemplative, thoughtful wisdom, the biggest, unexpected takeaway for me was how his authentic, genuine, and humble strong self came through.

In the first 30 seconds of our connection, I mentioned how honored I was to receive his wisdom to which he humbly replied: "Then this will be a quick two-minute conversation." As the conversation progressed, it became obvious that his love, kindness, and conviction were a perfect balance between soft and strong. His caring for me was palpable. I felt relevant, important, valued, respected, and empowered.

Truth be known, I would have done anything he asked, even if it meant to get on all fours and cut the grass with my teeth to smooth out the playing field. His vulnerability and listening skills drew me into the conversation, and I left feeling inspired and empowered to continue to write this book. He won the day by demonstrating with me, all of the impeccable traits and characteristics of the extraordinary leader that he is with his athletes. Similar to what you saw with the Steve Kerr Foreword, Coach Carroll's influence is widespread and significant. He truly cares and with that being said, it's time to segue into the next section of the book, LEADING WITH CARE—WIN THE DAY COACHING.

POWER OF INFLUENCE

The greatness of a man is not how much wealth he acquires, but in his integrity and his ability to affect those around him positively.

—*Bob Marley*

Arguably, the most challenging task that any coach will face is how to influence those individuals they lead in a positive, forward-moving manner. It is simple, yet not easy; your influence can create, or it can destroy; it can light a fire in an athlete's belly, or it can douse the flames. Accordingly, it is essential to understand that as a coach, your influence is powerful, yet never neutral.

I am always aware of this factor, when I compete, speak, teach, mentor, parent, or coach. My body language, my tone, my expressions, my gestures, my words all have an impact on how things transpire. So does my behavior.

One of my favorite things to do when I meet a team is to run up a hill together. By so doing, I demonstrate my willingness to experience what they do in training. I am leading by example, using the powerful influence I knowingly have. Ancient generals were considered influential, because they were willing to experience the same heat, cold, toil, hunger, thirst, and danger as their soldiers. As such, they were respected and admired because of this influential behavior.

When I enter a room full of coaches and athletes, I walk with a bounce, stand straight, keep my head up, look others in the eye, and smile. The message I'm sending is "things are under control, all is fine, it's all ok." As a coach, the more often you become aware of the power of your influence, the more you have a say in the outcome, the direction athletes will go, what they do, and how they feel. It is that simple.

When I am coaching one of my teams, I usually begin the sessions by inviting the athletes to "huddle up" close, forming a tight series of concentric circles (assuming there are 25 or so athletes on the team) around me. This action communicates togetherness, kindness, oneness, connectedness, and, most importantly, a sense of goodness. Then, I say the following: "I love being here; I love being with you. There's not another place I'd rather be or another group of athletes I'd rather be with in this moment than with you."

This spoken truth is visibly felt deeply by the entire group. They truly believe I care, and I do. I often will touch a shoulder and establish good eye contact with one person. Being aware of this power to influence others is to Win the Day. The athletes love it. We then go back to where we were, sitting, standing, and milling around. At that time, I have their full, undivided, respectful attention. By doing this, I set a positive, heart-directed caring tone for all the good work we will subsequently do together.

Implementation

When back into our circle, I love to involve the athletes and coaches in a powerful influential experience with their smart phones. I ask everyone to choose someone whom they deeply care about and text them a short message, expressing their care, love, and how important and valued they are to them. Once completed, I instruct them to turn off their devices for the next hour, giving them time to receive a response.

When the time is up, we go back to this exercise, turn the phones on and share the responses. Some are quite funny and even strange, but they all tell a story about the power we have to influence others in a positive way. On occasion, tears of joy are noticeable, and laughter is hardy, yet the caring and influences are remarkable. Try this with your group, and then have them communicate like this with each other, telling someone how important and valued they are to them and the team. Something else you can try with your team is to ask the following questions:

- What do you need to *start doing* that you're not doing in order to demonstrate the power of your influence in a positive way?
- What do you need to *stop doing* that you are doing in order to demonstrate the power of your influence in a positive way?

sirtravelalot/Shutterstock.com

Being aware of the power to influence others is to Win the Day.

The answer to these questions will provide information that is valuable in helping the athletes and staff to create positive shifts in the Win the Day culture. In fact, I inform the team that when we demonstrate such caring, positive action we actually do Win the Day. In fact, if he were alive today, I'm certain that Bob Marley would have said the words in the opening quote.

FEELINGS EQUAL FUNCTION

People will forget what you say; people will forget what you do.

But … they will never forget how you made them feel.

—Maya Angelou, Author, Poet

I love to open all of my talks, presentations, and conferences with this brilliant, insightful quote. I then proceed to explain how I go out of my way to help everyone feel welcomed as they enter the venue. I also get the audience to breathe deeply, relax, and feel present. I then make sure they feel important and valued (see the following section the RIVER Effect.) Subsequently, I quickly ask them if they ever do these things with their athletes, and if not, why not. The audience feels terrific and awesome. As a result, hopefully, they see the value of helping their athletes feel the same way. I tell them that when you feel welcomed, present, and valued, your performance improves. Accordingly, perhaps, these coaches may want to consider the benefits of using such an approach.

Most coaches and teachers believe that what they say and do is what really matters to others. Perhaps, we all would be wiser, if we focused on caring and helping others feel awesome. Why not? Every book I've read or written, every class or conference I've ever taken, every championship team I've ever helped has taught me a life-changing truth: feelings = function.

How we, as human beings, perform is directly related to how we feel. Think about it. The last time you felt tired, sad, depressed, distracted, confused, upset, insecure, stressed, uncertain, or miserable, how did you perform? Think about those moments, when you felt confident, energized, focused, happy, grateful, valued, respected, relevant, relaxed, and calm. No comparison, right? Creating environments where others feel good is how to Win the Day.

One of the first essential absolutes present in all championship cultures is the emphasis on how athletes and coaches feel and care for each other. To Win the Day, we must commit to helping others feel welcome, feel present, and feel cared for—caring being the single most important element of a winning culture. Fortunately, as coaches and athletes, we are able to make others feel good. As such, this factor is controllable.

Stas Rudenko/Shutterstock.com

One of the first essential absolutes present in all championship cultures is the emphasis on how athletes and coaches feel and care for each other.

Implementation

How can we best demonstrate our caring for each other? It's not about connecting my professional coaching head to your head. It's about connecting my human heart to your human heart to show how much I care for you. The following can help you to better understand this factor.

To connect my heart to yours, I imagine that I open the little door to my heart and become mindful of how I care for you. This "open door" policy reminds me to be caring, genuine, authentic, and vulnerable. I can then tell you, as I did in the section on Power of Influence: "I love being with you. There's not another team (person) I'd rather be with than you right now."

How does that make you feel? How do you think your athletes would feel if they heard this? Have you ever said this to an athlete? Why not? To not do this, there's a chance you could lose them. To do it, you increase the chance of getting your team to go the distance, to work harder, to be loyal, become mentally tougher and Win the Day. Performance on and off the court is all about feelings … how you feel is how you'll perform. It's really quite simple. When you care for your athletes like this, you are winning the day. In the words of actor Edward Albert, "The simple act of caring is heroic."

How you impact another, with regard to how they feel, can be determined by what I call the RIVER effect. What this is and how it works allows me to now segue into the next section, called the RIVER Effect.

RIVER EFFECT

I want to make sure that my guys feel valued, respected, relevant, and important.

When they do, magic happens, and they compete at higher levels.

—*Steve Kerr, Head Coach, Golden State Warriors*

Having kindness for all others is what the RIVER effect is truly about. The RIVER effect is a five-letter acronym that I use consistently as a reminder for extending kindness to all my relationships. It helps me to connect and care more deeply. I do what I can to help others feel the letters of RIVER and what they represent. In that regard, I want others to feel relevant, remarkable, important, inspired, valued, validated, empowered, excited, respected, and revered.

How do you behave, act, play, work, and compete, when you feel the river consuming you? This outcome entails caring, which is how you can Win the Day for yourself and for those you lead. When you remember and adopt the acronym RIVER, you can easily create amazing opportunities to inspire, empower, validate, and respect others. It becomes a mindful touchstone that, when used, increases the chances that others will be loyal, go the distance, work harder, and be mentally strong.

Implementation

The following are examples of a few statements that you can use to Win the Day and coach the RIVER effect with others.

- You're important to this team. We need your awesome efforts. (Relevant)
- I love your work ethic. It motivates all of us. (Remarkable)
- If you keep playing like that, you'll be one of the best athletes I've ever coached. (Inspired)
- We value your presence on this team. You bring out the best in everyone. (Valued)
- That last week of practice was one of your best thus far. (Validated)
- I want to give you permission to keep being a great leader. (Inspired)
- When you play and compete like that, you're being a true champion. (Empowered)
- Without you, we wouldn't be the great team we are. (Revered)
- I appreciate and love how much you give of yourself to your teammates. (Important)

Using the RIVER effect is easy. Simply be mindful of catching others doing something right and call positive attention to it. Watch as others feel significant and become open to going the distance. Author and leadership consultant, Mark Sanborn, claims that "the first job of leadership is to help people see their significance."

Current Middlebury College coach Bob Hansen, NCAA tennis coach of the decade (1990s) (while on the staff at UC Santa Cruz) has become an expert at marinating his athletes in the RIVER. Through diligent practice, Bob doles out words that inspire and value others on or off the court. His players love him, work extra hard, and compete like crazy for each other.

Golden State Warrior head coach, Steve Kerr, uses the RIVER concept on a daily basis and by so doing, gets the most from his players. Pete Carroll of the Seattle Seahawks is always looking for an opportunity to demonstrate similar caring strategies that help his athletes feel respected and important. I told him about the RIVER acronym, and he subsequently agreed how helpful that is in bringing out the best in others.

Cindy Timchal, winningest lacrosse coach ever, for men or women, has adopted and adapted the RIVER effect to her coaching style. When she's mindful of using it, she notices that there is a major "buy-in" to her systems. She bathes her athletes in the RIVER and then notices the tsunami, concerning how "the athletes are super willing to put it all out on the field."

While I didn't realize it at the time, in retrospect, my first and only meeting with the iconic men's basketball coach at the University of North Carolina, Dean Smith, showed me that he was brilliant at using the RIVER effect, even though he hadn't thought about it in this way. He was the kind of leader who, through deep, genuine caring, would Win the Day. Following an intimate 45-minute meeting together, I felt so inspired, valued, and important that I committed myself to writing my book, *Coaching With Heart.*

The substance of water is used widely as a metaphor in Eastern Taoist cultures for guiding and leading in a strong and fluid way. I often use it as a way to describe desired motion during athletic events, such as basketball, soccer, and lacrosse.

Tao is often referred to as the Watercourse Way. In fact, it refers to the fluid flow of nature, and this flow of water is often used as a principal metaphor by Lao-Tzu and other Chinese scholars. For a Taoist, water is the basis of all life, given that it nurtures and nourishes all living things. Thus the choice I've made to establish the RIVER effect and like all water, it becomes the bedrock of a strong culture, nurturing all those who thrive and expand in its awesome flow.

The word RIVER is not only an appropriate acronym for focusing on caring for others, it is also a wonderful metaphor for how to lead and coach a championship culture. There is a Buddhist expression that says, "from little streams, come big rivers." The big victories and championships for coaches are usually the outcome of having done all the little things, like attention to feelings and building healthy, functional relationships.

The big victories and championships for coaches are usually the outcome of having done all the little things, like attention to feelings and building healthy, functional relationships.

The river is soft, yet strong; it wears away rock carving its path along the journey to the ocean, as it lights up cities. On the other hand, it is the softest substance you can lay your hands on. Like the river, coaches in a championship culture must be strong and demanding, establish boundaries, set limits, create a path, and yet, be kind, respectful, affirming, loving, and caring. Demanding and loving … soft and strong … are, indeed, compatible. Furthermore, like the mighty river that gives itself to the land and mother ocean, the greatest coaches are servants, leaders who give and serve those to whom they are responsible.

Before this book transitions into the next session, THE RELATIONSHIP GAME, I want to remind all leaders, coaches, mentors, and parents, that the more we make valuing others a priority, the more we help others feel relevant, important, inspired, and respected. As such, the more abundance we all experience, the more we Win the Day.

THE RELATIONSHIP GAME

Extraordinary Win the Day coaching begins and ends with one word: Relationship.

It is the single most vital aspect to successful coaching. Top coaches have figured out that the way to get ahead is not necessarily to win games, but to win the relationship game.

—Bob Hansen, Head Men's Tennis Coach, Middlebury College

Most coaching education programs devote much of their time helping students to master the technical aspects of a specific sport. Truth be known, much of athletics are drowning in a sea of Xs and Os information, primarily supplied through the Internet. What really separates the good coaches from the great ones, however, is not a brilliant, tactical game plan; it's the relationship game plan.

My personal and professional relationship with iconic Hall of Fame coaches like Dean Smith, Steve Kerr, Phil Jackson, Anson Dorrance, Cindy Timchal, and others has convinced me that while the Xs and Os game is important, it is the relationship game, the caring of others, that drives and sustains success in championship team cultures. In the process, I have discovered what, arguably, are the three most highly effective powers to mastering the relationship game in sports and life, as well. As you continue to read, notice how all three elements relate to the RIVER effect. In that regard, the transformational questions that are presented are meant to help you get started and coach to that powerful element to win the relationship game, as well as Win the Day.

Implementation

❑ Power of Influence

Having previously addressed this powerful factor, I will summarize its importance in this instance. If you are to be effective and Win the Day as a coach, you must be totally aware of the power of your influence. You can either light up your environment and the life of another, or cast it into darkness. The more mindful you are of this factor, the more say you have in the outcome.

You consciously send signals, like the RIVER effect, to build caring and connection with others. Caring and connection are the most important elements in culture success. As such, you make a substantial effort to send signals that you hope become part of the oxygen.

At this point, take your cell phone and send a signal to a friend, a short text, helping them to feel cared for, relevant, important, and how valued they are to your life. Then, happily wait for the response. Combine the two previous questions from the chapter on Power of Influence to assist you with implementing your influence: What do you need to *start doing* or *stop doing* to demonstrate your power of influence? Think about how the RIVER effect can help you answer this query.

❑ Power of Environment

Winning the day is also about creating mentally, emotionally, and spiritually safe environments that show caring. By safe, I mean to be free, with no fear about failure, mistakes, setbacks, or loss, as well as being ridiculed, insulted, or messing up. I go out of my way to make sure others are safe. I employ small, subtle, non-verbal signals and cues, such as touching a shoulder, establishing eye contact, thumbs up, listening, validating, being vulnerable, and humble, as signals to help make environments safer and more caring.

Win the Day, by implementing the RIVER effect, can help others feel safe. When others feel important, valued, and respected, they feel cared for and open their hearts, giving you permission to step in, so that you can connect more deeply and teach them that they can be extraordinary. If an athlete's heart is not open, no coaching can take place. You can only do your work, when the environment is safe, fear is mitigated, and hearts are opened.

The following is a transformational question that can help you to implement the power of environment more safety: What do you need to *start doing* or *stop doing* to create more safety in your environment? When you execute the answer, you Win the Day.

Motortion Films/Shutterstock.com

If an athlete's heart is not open, no coaching can take place.

❑ Power of Love

For me, winning the day is about winning your heart. I fight for your heart by using the greatest success strategy ever—LOVE. Coach John Wooden, winner of 11 national championships in NCAA men's basketball at UCLA, had something noteworthy to say about love. When he retired, he was asked by the media what he believed to be the reason for his extraordinary success. He simply told the interviewers that there was a lot of love in his coaching. Wooden, along with the other 11 Hall of Fame coaches contributing to this book, believe that they Win the Day by loving and caring for those individuals whom they coach.

For example, Coach Pete Carroll told me that the centerpiece to his coaching makeup originates from love. He allows himself to feel that love for his athletes, and they, in turn, feel it in all aspects of their work. Coach K at Duke University often speaks about the importance of athletes knowing you care deeply for them. He develops strong loving relationships by letting the players know he believes in them. Coaching, to him, is all about caring relationships. Coach Phil Jackson, 13 time world champion, claims that it takes several critical factors to win an NBA championship, the most essential ingredient being love in your coaching and love throughout the team. Coach Steve Kerr of the Golden State Warriors does not hesitate to express his love for his players. During a recent game after a time-out, the camera focused on Steve saying "I love you" to Steph Curry, as Curry returned to the court.

A word of caution, however. If you're coaching youngsters, such expressions could be misconstrued these days, with all of the incidents of child sex abuse occurring. In reality, we all need to be a bit cautious and judicious with the words we choose. On the other hand, that doesn't have to stop you from expressing your love through the RIVER and by how you treat others with kindness, compassion, and respect.

While it's easy to care for and love the good players, you must also care for and love the more challenging ones, as well. I have struggled with this factor in my coaching. What helps me to be a good coach is to remember that the challenging athletes are, like me, human beings. Furthermore, I also remind myself that these youngsters, unlike me, may be insecure, immature, and very fearful. They're afraid of messing up, letting others down, failing, looking silly, losing, making mistakes, not being good enough, or even getting injured. Their response to this mindset is to withdraw, hold back, and look for an exit strategy.

You can Win the Day and help them to Win the Day by finding ways to baptize them in the RIVER. For example, make your athletes feel like they are the most important people in your life … like they are your superstars. Place them above winning. Give them what you'd want others to give you, when you are afraid.

When they feel loved and cared for, magic happens. They open their hearts, allowing you to coach. In turn, there's a feeling of liberation, of being set free. So, love them with all your heart, soul, and mind. While you're at it, love and care for yourself too. It's hard to love another, when we don't love ourselves.

The following strategies are specific methods that I use with coaches, like you, to help them win through the relationship game:

❑ The "Oneness Rule"

This rule is designed to help you to connect and care. When I was a college student, I struggled with getting good grades. I recall getting mostly Cs in my major, English literature. There was one course, however, in which the professor graded one of my papers an A+. He looked me in the eyes, and I remember what he said to me to this day, because it changed my life, "You're a terrific writer."

Here I am, many years later, making a difference in the lives of others, having written 13 books because of that one comment by one person on one given day. It helped me feel valued and important. As a consequence, I now Win the Day, doing good things for so many others.

I suggest that you use the Oneness Rule strategy in the following way. You and your staff choose ONE athlete each, ONE day at a time, and give that person ONE positive comment about either something they do or who they are. The RIVER effect will work well for this activity. Personally, I like to catch an athlete doing something right, blow the whistle, and point it out to the entire team.

❑ Electronic Messaging

I try to make good use of the electronic age, being a huge proponent of sending positive, upbeat, caring emails and texts to my players. In a similar vein, Anson Dorrance, head coach of the North Carolina's women's soccer team, tells me he loves to leave notes in the lockers of players, expressing his good feeling about them, both as significant athletes and awesome contributors to the Win the Day culture.

❑ L.U.V. Strategy

This strategy works wonders in executing the power of love. It is another acronym, one that stands for listen, understand, validate.

L is for "listen." I let the players talk, and I listen intently to their issues or concerns. I notice how athletes respect coaches who listen to them. Listening, it turns out, is one of the more important keys to heart-based leadership. (See the next section on Listening.)

U refers to "understand," through the process of asking questions. Accordingly, I proceed to ask basic, direct questions, based on what I've heard, helping the players to gain clarity through their answers, as well as enabling them to feel valued by my close connection to their important words.

Finally, V is for validate. Everyone wants to feel special and important. As such, the validation process helps in this regard. Validation gives definition to the coaching environment, helping to inspire and empower the athlete to commit, persevere, compete, and comply with the team culture. It reinforces any and all success experiences, helping an athlete to stay on track and connected. I may say something like: "I appreciate your open, candid remarks about the team. We value your input. You're important to our success." Or, "I am so happy you brought that to my attention. I'm glad you are part of this team." Know that these vital three elements—L.U.V.—are interdependent and dance together with no particular order.

When you develop this level of influence with your athletes, they will begin to trust their fearless leader. The way it works is very straightforward. When a player feels heard, understood, and validated, the athlete feels safer. When feeling safer, a feeling of trust exists. With more trust comes more openness. When an athlete is more open, learning increases, and performance improves. Accordingly, the more an athlete opens to you, not only will you have more influence, you will also be more effective with all those whom you lead. In other words, simply put: no trust, no relationship.

With a strong, positive relationship, you can ask your athletes to do all it takes to improve, and they will oblige accordingly, provided you let them know that you have confidence in their ability to do it. They need to know, also, that if they fail, you will be there to help them to learn from the setback, as well as will coach them to eventually master their skills. I tell my athletes that I am here for them and will always have their best interest in mind.

The following is a transformative question that you should ask yourself to help gain this power: What do you need to *start doing* or *stop doing* to demonstrate more love in your culture?

The power of love, as a concept for team culture, is not new. Over 2,000 years ago, the Taoist book of change, *I CHING*, made it clear that leaders must care for, support, and love those who are led in order to build a unified and powerful culture. Sun-Tzu, in *The Art of War*, alludes to the value of generals loving their troops, as one would love a child. By so doing, you Win the Day.

LISTENING WITH THE HEART

Be a good listener; it makes the person who's speaking to you feel loved, cared for, and worthy of being heard.

—Dr. Wayne Dyer, Self-Help Author and Motivational Speaker

Coach Cindy Timchall, iconic coach of the Navy women's lacrosse team, believes that listening, more than any other coaching skill, is what inspires and empowers her athletes. According to her, it's the most powerful tool to demonstrate caring for athletes.

In a recent interview with sports psychologist Greg Dale, Coach Mike Krzyzewski mentioned how he believes "you show someone you care about them by being willing to listen to them. There is no better way." He goes on to state that "there couldn't be any time better spent than listening" to your athletes, staff, family, and friends. When we listen with an open heart, we Win the Day.

It has been said that the person who listens with an open heart understands. Listening is one of the most crucial skills a coach can develop. Because so many of us feel that we need to talk in order to teach, listening is often overlooked. What I have observed over the years is that the very popular, well-liked coaches are, indeed, good listeners.

John Wooden was a good listener. In his words, "listen to those under your supervision. Really listen. Don't act as though you're listening and let it go in one ear and out the other." It has been observed that three out of four leaders and coaches will interrupt their staff and athletes on average, within 15 seconds of the start of a conversation. Such a practice precludes you from truly learning from others what you need to know in order to do your best work. How can you build a strong relationship in this way?

As Wayne Dyer alludes to in the opening quote, listening is an extraordinary way to demonstrate caring, respect, love, and integrity. Learning and teaching are more easily and joyfully exchanged through good listening, as well. It is a way to make the athlete feel wanted, valued, worthwhile, and understood. Isn't this exactly what all coaches desire for their athletes? Those we lead feel the same way. Furthermore, what better tool to use in order to develop solid relationships … and, therefore, Win the Day.

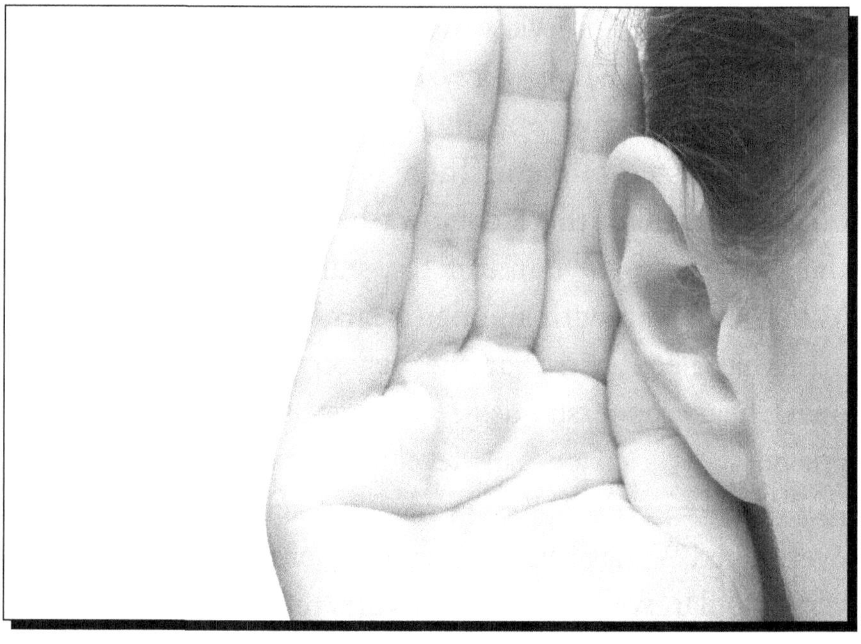

Voronin76/Shutterstock.com

Learning and teaching are more easily and joyfully exchanged through good listening.

Implementation

To develop a listener's approach to your coaching, there are certain steps to take on that path. First of all, you must be willing to take the time to hear what is to be said. You need to have the heart-set that makes you eager to help. When the athlete talks about their feelings, you must convey acceptance by listening with your heart, as well as your ears. You don't have to agree with them, but you must accept those feelings as spoken by a human being who trusts and respects you.

Rarely, do any of us get the opportunity to learn listening skills. The following simple skills will help you to engage your athletes, improve your relationships, solve problems, make good decisions, and create environments that are safe and more productive:

- *Door openers* – a way to invite the other person to say more, in a noncommittal way: "I see;" "Really;" "Interesting;" "Is that so?;" "You don't say"
- *Stepping inside the door* – invitation for the other person to go further and be more explicit: "Tell me more;" "I'd like to hear about it;" "Let's discuss it"
- *Keeping the door wide open* – this strategy is the most effective of the three.
  - ✓ Try to understand what the sender is feeling or means.
  - ✓ Put into your own words and feedback what you believe you hear; "It sounds like ...;" "What I hear you saying…;" "Correct me if I'm wrong…"

For listening to be effective, give feedback for *only* what you feel is the sender's message, nothing more, nothing less. Try not to interrupt. Limit distractions and silence your phone. Use good eye contact and positive body language. Do not warn, moralize, lecture, judge, blame, or criticize. With experience, you will grow more direct and intuitive. For now, simply use what another says and put it in your own words. At first, it may feel contrived or awkward. That's okay; just do it anyway and tell others that it helps you to understand better.

These simple yet powerful skills will not only just help your athletes to perform at higher levels, they will also move them to a spirit of unparalleled loyalty. As a result, you will gain their compliance, as you direct them into areas of greater development personally, as well as athletically.

Wise leaders immerse with others, refusing to act judgmentally. In this way, everyone opens ears, hearts, minds, making them more able to understand the needs of others.

—*Tao Te Ching, No. 49*

MINDFUL SELF-AWARENESS

When you know both yourself, as well as your competitors, you are never in danger. Know yourself but not others, and you have half a chance of winning.

Knowing neither puts you in position to lose.

—Sun-Tzu, The Art of War

I read in Bill George's book *Authentic Leadership* that the Stanford Graduate School of Business's Advisory Council was asked to recommend the most valuable, important capability for leaders to develop and their answer was mindful self-awareness.

For the purpose of Win the Day cultures, it is imperative that you have a strong sense of mindful self-awareness and apply that in all aspects of your life. Being aware of your strengths and weaknesses will assist you in making good decisions that fit skintight over your spirit, who you truly are. It will help you to have clear vision going forward in your life, which positions you for great success in all your endeavors. Self-knowledge is the true secret to helping you Win the Day consistently.

Self-awareness is an accurate appraisal of who you are, a measure of your physical, mental, spiritual, and emotional fitness. It takes courage to take this inventory of personal struggles, obstacles, and fears to determine what is needed in order to transcend your limitations. In addition, such awareness is a hedge against selling yourself short and running the risk of feeling inferior.

According to tennis star Billy Jean King, "Self-awareness is probably the most important thing toward being a champion" … as well as a great coach. Defined, self-awareness is to know your shortcomings and strong points; acknowledge them; and decide what you can and cannot change; and take action. It is the ability to notice all of it, learn and change. Stephen Curry reminds us that self-awareness demands deep personal honesty. "It comes from asking and answering hard questions."

Implementation

When I work with teams, I have a few pointed, direct, life-changing questions to begin the process, as suggested by Stephen Curry. Take your time, no rush; all answers are personal and correct:

- Who has been the most influential, inspiring person/leader/coach in your life?
  - ✓ What three traits from this person that you don't have would you'd like to have?
  - ✓ What three specific actions can you take to help you consistently embody these?
  - ✓ Write these three actions on index cards, one per card, as affirmations. For example: "I demonstrate my love for my team each day by using the RIVER effect;" and "I model integrity by making sure I do what I say I'll do."

marekuliasz/Shutterstock.com

Self-awareness is to know your shortcomings and strong points; acknowledge them; and decide what you can and cannot change; and take action.

- What do you like MOST about yourself? What do you like LEAST about yourself?
  - ✓ Take your list of LEAST, and then write the specific steps you can undertake in order to change these.
  - ✓ Write affirmations as you did in the first exercise. For example, you like least that you are a poor listener. Say this: "I listen with open, non-judgmental heart when being spoken to by my athletes."
- What do you need to start (or stop) doing in order to be more caring, a better listener, better connected, more empowering, and more present?
  - ✓ Write your answers on index cards and add them to the deck with the aforementioned.
- What is a defining moment in your life, and how did it change you?
- If you could change last year, what would you do differently?
  - ✓ What specific actions would you take to make these changes?

Involved in the process of personal awareness is the idea of creating positive self-images and self-talk, pictures and words that clearly spell out your strengths, while creating a vision of what is possible. Replace old, worn-out negative thoughts and messages with up-beat positive phrases and affirmations that are forward-moving and facilitate your upward development as a heart-directed coach. This activity becomes an ongoing, updating process to avoid listening to the deleterious chatter of negativity. Following the advice of the Tao *I Ching*, the Taoist book of change, you should exercise unrelenting discipline over your thought patterns. Cultivate only productive attitudes.

Every year, there is a huge coaching conference that my business, Way of Champions, conducts, gathering well over a hundred coaches from four or more continents. I can tell you that the topic of self-awareness and the subsequent questions completed as exercises draws considerable positive attention. It's astounding how many seminarians come away feeling better about who they are and who they possibly could become. I tell them how a coach's life unexamined is not worth living.

Personally, I am on a path to being the best coach/person I can be. When I examine the "why factor" of my coaching, aside from wanting to make a difference in the lives of others and change the status quo of sports is the mission to master my craft—to be the best version of "Jerry" I can be. After several decades with this mission, I estimate that I'm only halfway there. It's so much fun and so meaningfully satisfying. Try it!

Self-awareness is the key to your success. Many of us think we know ourselves, but believe me, we don't go on a journey of self-exploration. You will be amazed at the wonderful person you will discover. The journey to knowing self is a lifelong pursuit. It never stops, and you therefore have infinite opportunities for amazement.

—Mary-Frances Winters, Strategic Planner, Diversity Maven CEO, Winters Group

LEADING AUTHENTICALLY

The concept of authenticity is a lifelong search to be yourself and be able to demonstrate that self-discovery every day.

—Coach Pete Carroll

As you read in the section on *The Relationship Game*, if a coach is to be effective they must be authentic, vulnerable, and have love in their heart. This set of attributes is one of the best ways to show caring in your culture. When you demonstrate these valuable traits, you set the stage to Win the Day, as a true leader caring for others.

Speaking to me recently, Hall of Fame Coach Bob Hansen stated emphatically that being authentic for him meant creating the energy that adds value to others. Bob calls it leading from your basic core values, such as integrity, courage, vulnerability, and compassion.

Being authentic for Coach Phil Jackson is how you build strong relationships. Furthermore, as you've witnessed, winning the relationship game is the key to successful culture.

Anson Dorrance, head coach of 22-time national champions Carolina women's soccer, agrees that authenticity builds solid relationships. He told me how critical it is in the building of connection with others, staff, and athletes.

Cindy Timchal, head women's lacrosse coach at Navy—eight-time champions—says, unequivocally, that being authentic enables her athletes to feel valued and important. I've worked with Cindy for over 20 years … she is herself, she's approachable. You can't help but want to be near her positive, infectious energy and vulnerable laughter.

In a recent conversation with Pete Carroll, he mentioned that the concept of personal authenticity is a life search to be yourself and be able to demonstrate that self-discovery every day. To him, being authentic is the ability to empower yourself to communicate your uncompromising values. He's a believer, as is Bob Hansen, that authenticity is about leading from core principles.

What all these iconic coaches have in common is their belief that their success in their championship cultures, over a sustained period of time, is directly correlated to being authentic leaders.

When I observe authentic coaches, they have several common traits: they are fully awake and aware, have the ability to let go (see section on being happy), embrace a higher purpose, are compassionate and passionate, are self-aware, understand the power of their influence, have a sense of humor, laugh at themselves, and are unwilling to compromise their core values. This scenatio is authenticity in leadership.

Microgen/Shutterstock.com

Winning the relationship game is the key to successful culture.

Implementation

The following are examples of some of the ways you can demonstrate being authentic: establish eye contact, listen, touch others on the shoulder, or pat them on the back. Just be you and let your coach/leader role fade into the background. You can then become an authentic human being, not a "role." I notice how many coaches play a role, fearing that if they don't, they may lose control. As a result, they hide, pose, posture, and play the part and, in the process, become less authentic and vulnerable. Playing a role also creates separation and makes connection nearly impossible.

To be authentic and vulnerable, you must "take off the mask" and have the courage to show up and be seen. For me, it is a practice I engage in every time an opportunity is presented. When I do this, I have the chance to connect more deeply with others. Some of the ways I take the mask off is to admit I was wrong: "boy, I really screwed that up." I will tell others that I have failed greatly in my lifetime. Or, when presenting an idea, I'll say, "tell me what's wrong with this idea," or "maybe you can punch holes in this concept."

Being vulnerable and authentic is having the courage to be wrong, to not be perfect, and to be willing to admit you were wrong. It is the willingness to let go of who you think you should be in order to authentically be who you are. Being vulnerable and authentic is a sure way to show you care. When being authentic, your athletes and peers have greater respect and love for you, and your guidance will be embraced more fully. As a speaker to large audiences, when I'm open, authentic, genuine, and vulnerable, the sense of caring and connection is deep

Being vulnerable and authentic is having the courage to be wrong, to not be perfect, and to be willing to admit you were wrong.

and their response is riveting. This is my *secret sauce* that helps raise my effectiveness and discover my full human capacity as a coach, athlete, person.

What I have learned, over the years, is that when I put my role aside and am myself, being vulnerable, present, transparent, and authentic, I am much more effective and have a subtle transformational effect on whomever I coach and lead. I am most powerful, most influential, and most happy, when I am being completely myself. Furthermore, the nice thing about that is that I am not superior to anyone, nor inferior. I refuse to take myself too seriously, which shows a level of self-caring as well.

What I notice about so many individuals who "play the role" of leader-coach is that they do take themselves and life much too seriously. When this situation occurs, the spontaneity, joy, lightheartedness, and humor become invisible (assuming these traits ever existed). In the absence of such authenticity, true, effective, inspirational leadership is not possible.

Humorless, joyless leadership is an oxymoron. Basically, the "role" itself begins to define you as a "human doing;" you lose touch with the real you, a "human being" having a leadership experience, not a leader having a human experience. If you lose yourself in the "role of leader-coach," you run the risk of not having authentic relationships with those individuals whom you guide. Remember that extraordinary leadership/coaching is all about caring and connection in a safe, trustworthy, respectful, human environment. Authentic, emotionally engaging relationships are impossible to create, when you get too self-absorbed.

kcube/Shutterstock.com

Humorless, joyless leadership is an oxymoron.

The way to ensure authenticity is through mindful awareness. Be mindful of how you talk, and interact and treat those you guide, if you desire to be influential. Ask yourself: is your role and the way you relate to others causing distance, making you feel superior, preventing emotional engagement? Is it a block to being transparent, when transparency actually facilitates the power of authenticity?

There are many consistent, sustainable successful teams that I've had the honor of influencing. The common denominator of all these championship cultures is their authentic leadership, coaches who lead adaptively from their core values. These individuals are who they are—human beings serving others to be something other than extraordinary.

Speaking of core values, this occasion is the perfect time to segue into Part III. Read on.

PART III

IDENTIFYING PERSONAL VALUES—Win the Day Character

If you are authentic with your team, and your daily routine at practice and games and team meetings reflect your personal core values, well, then, now you're going somewhere.

Now, you're building a culture. Now, you're coaching.

—Steve Kerr, Head Coach, Golden State Warriors

In this, Part III of the *Win the Day* journey, you are introduced to and invited to cultivate personal values of a leader's heart and soul. Your core values are the emotional and spiritual foundational building blocks that define who you are, what you do, how you do it, and why. They keep you anchored to what really matters and drive success in your culture. These "non-negotiables" are the essence of your coaching and, by association, are a reflection of what you and your program represents. They are the standard by which personal excellence is measured in the coaching game.

Being a coach requires you to open deeply to your innate nature, take a look at what you have, and decide what's needed, in order to lead others to places they never dreamed possible. These personal values will help you understand that soft is, indeed, strong in our relationships. Universal ancient warrior qualities, such as compassion, courage, gratefulness, honesty, selflessness and more, will enable you and your athletes to learn to go beyond human emotional and spiritual blockages, and strengthen the bond and connectedness of all, when you desire to inspire. This part of the book is designed to help you make sense out of what you do and why you do it. It will inspire and empower you, as well as your evolving athletes, to address conflict, doubt, and develop the self in the process.

These values are transcendent, taking you to places deep inside you, in order to be more mindful of the needs of others, as you travel with others to greater spiritual and emotional depths. They will provide a clearer sense about your relationships with your athletes from the inside out. This section addresses a special group of values that help everyone to develop, in a word, character. Keep in mind that it takes time and experience to develop these character values.

In the words of J.C. Watts, American politician, clergyman, and renowned athlete, "Everyone tries to define this thing called character. It's not hard. Character is doing what's right when nobody's looking." Do you and your athletes do this? I could use some work on this. I like to lean on the wisdom of Coach John Wooden for his view about character: "a true athlete should have character, not be a character. Some believe that sports build character. I believe that sports reveal character. A person of character is trustworthy and honest."

CHARACTER: Doing the Right Thing

Character is what you really are. A person of character is trustworthy and honest.

Reputation is what people say you are.

—John Wooden, Former Head Men's Basketball Coach, UCLA

Character is a virtue and a value, something that is indicative of moral and ethical strength, goodness, and personal *integrity*. It is the keystone to being a great coach, person, or athlete. Integrity, as it relates to character, is the refusal to "sell out" on the true inner self, regardless of what situations are present in life. The Chinese characters for *integrity* put this value in perspective. Translated, they mean: "wholeness and refinement of character, with a commitment to stand up for personal principles." The *Tao Te Ching*, the ancient Chinese book of leadership, talks about how doing the right thing is strength of character. Quoting this tome of wisdom:

Hold to your ethics and principles.
Stand strongly for what you hold true.
Believe in your true self, without compromises.
Trust in the power within yourself and use it.
Act in concert with your dreams and visions.

Tao sages state that when people are true and honest to themselves, they hit upon what is right, find what is good, understand what's to be known, and create a life of harmony, happiness, satisfaction, and success.

Only by being true and honest to your inner self can you fulfill your coaching dreams and those of your athletes. When you are out of touch with your inner self, you feel fear. Accordingly, you must maintain your integrity at all costs by identifying and cultivating your deep-rooted values. Only by knowing what your values are can character be developed. You allow others to control your thoughts or beliefs and make you feel inferior, when you act dishonestly about these values. What would it be like if you acted from a place of deep self-truth to connect with the same deep truth with your teams? If being deeply honest threatens this relationship, do you really have a healthy thing going?

Your words and actions are the manifestation of your *character*, who you really are, as John Wooden states. In other words, if you want your athletes to trust you, you must be a trustworthy person. Don't promise more than you can deliver, and don't say things you don't mean. Such mixed messages confuse athletes. For example, college coaches sign recruits by promising that these individuals will be impact players in the program and will get plenty of minutes. However, once an athlete is committed, if it turns out that a particular player is more valuable to the staff and team in a role that is different than what was promised, the staff will use the athlete as they see fit, regardless of the promise.

Better for a coach to say how much they would like to coach an athlete and state a vision for the player, assuming everything works out as expected. It's tempting to promise the moon, but no one can predict the future. Promise, instead, that you and the staff will work diligently to create opportunities for the athlete to grow and improve.

When athletes see cracks in the dam of a coach's *character*, and, by extension, the program's integrity, they may choose various routes to safety. Some will remain with the program but "check out" emotionally, making it unlikely that they'll live up to their athletic potential, while in that particular environment. Others choose to leave the program for the promise of something better elsewhere.

Implementation

To help you to develop stronger *character* traits, answer the following questions:

- What coach demonstrates the *character* traits you most desire?
- What specifically are these traits?
- What can you specifically do today to demonstrate one or all of these traits?

When you've completed this exercise, write the behavior out on cards, as you would affirmations, and read them to yourself each day, before going to work. You can also have your team do a similar exercise but be sure to change the first question to "which athlete …"

To help you in your *character* development as a coach, employ the wisdom of your team. Ask them to anonymously answer these questions:

- What are your best traits as a coach?
- What aspects of your coaching do you need to improve?

Look for patterns in the responses. Is there one trait that several respondents cited as your strongest point? Is there one trait that stands out—a unanimously agreed-on trait? If over half of the athletes respond with the same complaint or criticism, you should definitely be concerned.

As such, you can decide to take concrete steps to change this trait, since it's likely a hindrance to effective coaching. By conducting such a survey, you communicate your openness to improvement and change, a strong character trait in itself.

There is no particular combination of *character* traits that makes a coach great. You must do what is comfortable for you, and even experiment from time to time to determine what is and is not comfortable. New coaches find that they experiment quite a bit with different styles. In time, they learn what a good fit is for them. Consistency in their coaching style then follows.

Several coaches I have worked with attribute their coaching success to being true to their basic nature—whether that means being shy, opinionated, strong-willed, talkative, direct, or humorous—and then expressing this nature through *character* traits they know to be right, such as honesty, fairness, kindness, respect, and patience.

BrandonKleinVideo/Shutterstock.com

There is no particular combination of character traits that makes a coach great.

The following are some of the main tenets of character. Perhaps, you could add others. Jot down next to each trait (and any others you have added) an example of how you demonstrate it in your daily coaching. If you don't currently demonstrate a particular attribute in your coaching, how could you do so in your coaching and other aspects of your life? Make your own list and place it where you will see it every day.

Consistency ______________________________
Courage ______________________________
Dependability______________________________
Fairness ______________________________
Flexibility ______________________________
Gratefulness______________________________
Honesty ______________________________
Humility ______________________________
Joyful ______________________________
Kindness ______________________________
Openness ______________________________
Patience ______________________________
Positivity ______________________________
Respectful ______________________________
Selflessness ______________________________
Vulnerability______________________________

All of the coaches to which I've referred in this book have risen to the top of their professions to become champions. Without a strong sense of *character*, however, it would be difficult for them to remain in that position. As a coach, you are challenged with *character* issues every day. As such, you need to find innovative ways to deal with those challenges. Find other individuals, if you can, who will offer support for your stance. On the other hand, remember that you can't run a popularity contest. You will almost always meet with some opposition. If you follow your heart and stick to what you intuitively know is right, you will be on the proper path.

As you can see, the cultivation of strong *character* is the foundation of an effective culture. Without core ethical qualities, you run the risk of tearing yourself down, instead of building your team up. Use strong *character* to create a solid team bond and an environment in which greatness and success can flourish. Such an environment will be greatly enhanced by the use of effective communication skills that will enable you to develop quality relationships with your athletes. When this happens, you Win the Day.

COMPASSION: Generosity of an Open Heart

Compassion is often the only remedy when someone assaults our bodies, minds, and spirits.

No one can completely take away our pain. But they can share it with us.

—Joseph Marshall III, Lakota Historian, Writer, and Teacher

One of the Golden State Warriors Win the Day core values is *compassion*. Steve Kerr states that "*the most powerful leaders and cultures in the world are the ones who have an awareness of compassion for others.*"

Steve Kerr played on Phil Jackson's world championship Chicago Bulls team, where his soul was marinated in the juices of this core value. He also experienced *compassion* values with head coach Gregg Popovich, as a player on the San Antonio Spurs. I've talked with Kerr about *compassion* as a cultural value. He believes, as does Jackson, that players respond wholeheartedly to such an environment by their actions, such as when they play and don't, and understanding their roles, as well as understanding each other. Being a great communicator, Kerr actively demonstrates his understanding of his players' concerns, issues, and what matters most to them. Because of this approach, all the Warriors feel that they are valued, that they are important, and that they count, regardless of their talents.

Phil Jackson, associated with 13 championship NBA teams, claims it was the core value of *compassion* that allowed his teams to experience extraordinary success. In his bestseller *Sacred Hoops*, Jackson talks about the importance of the players treating each other with the same care and respect you give yourself. When we can do that, "we begin to see that we all share basic human struggles, desires, and dreams. With awareness of this, the barriers between us gently give way and we begin to understand that we're part of something larger than ourselves."

Jackson also talks about the need to open his heart to comprehend situations from his athletes' point of view, to practice selfless *compassion.* He considers compassion as the most important treasure of his coaching and culture. It is non-negotiable. Both he and his guys used *compassion* to Win the Day.

Pete Carroll, head coach of the Seattle Seahawks, demonstrates an intuitive sense of *compassion* in his championship culture. *Compassion* is not a concept that's often discussed in the NFL, but it is one of the characteristics that the Seahawks players most admire about Coach Carroll. It enabled them to connect deeply, connection being a vital element in successful cultures.

Buddhism's teaching of *compassion* is extremely compelling. The Buddhists' culture is intent on cultivating an open, unlimited heart toward humanity. The Chinese ancient book of leadership, *Tao Te Ching*, states that "leaders whose positions are lasting are those who are most compassionate; when two armies meet, the one with *compassion* is the one who tastes victory."

Such thought is extremely relevant in the current world of sports. Where there is *compassion*, there is courage within, giving a person a sense of comfort and security, knowing that if risks are taken, regardless of outcome, all will be fine. For example, *compassion* helps you to not worry about mistakes, failure, or loss. When setbacks occur, the core value of *compassion* helps you to learn from failure and move on. You get less tense, less tight, and less stressed, knowing you'll be encouraged to learn from mistakes, rather than be chastised. Furthermore, because you're more calm and relaxed, you actually raise your level of performance. *Compassion* empowers you to be brave, fearless, tenacious, and relentless, as well as strengthen your connection.

Implementation

In Native American cultures, *compassion* for your opponent or enemies is a value they embrace openly. Following a national championship in the Spirit of the Lakota Nation, I encouraged the victorious athletes to talk with the losing team immediately and express their understanding about the agony of defeat. I asked the athletes: How does your

Laszlo Szirtesi/Shutterstock.com

When setbacks occur, the core value of compassion helps you to learn from failure and move on.

opponent feel right now? That opened their hearts. They went to them, embraced, and thanked them for their courageous and fearless battle, as well as playing all out with heart. You could feel the camaraderie between the teams strengthen. As a result, the loss in the moment seemed somewhat easier to digest. The team and the players had plenty of time to focus and celebrate by ourselves away from the arena.

Two years later, this same opponent defeated us in the national championship and they showed similar *compassion* for us as we did for them two years earlier.

Nancy Stevens, the head coach of three-time national champion University of Connecticut women's field hockey program, talks openly about *compassion* in her winning culture by using the phrase, "You are enough." With regard to those words, she stated:

"Before we began the 2017 preseason, I put these three simple words on the board in our team room. I wanted the tone to be one of compassion. Many players feel that they may not be strong enough, fast enough, or good enough to meet the challenges that lie ahead. These feelings can create anxiety and a lack of self-compassion. By reassuring our incoming players that they were, in fact, enough, we were able to reduce their anxiety levels, which resulted in more productive preseason practice sessions.

"Walking into the locker room several months later, before the 2017 national championship game, you could feel the high energy in that room. I wrote once again those three words on the locker room board: 'You are enough.' I could see the body language of our team immediately change, as the anxiety drained from their bodies. We went on to win the national championship by playing our best game of the season—relaxed, confident, and focused in the moment."

Missy Foote, winner of four national championship games as head women's lacrosse coach at Middlebury College, shares her wisdom about the value of *compassion* in a champion culture in the following statement:

"The most important quality we can share within a team (or community or family) is to value one another's differences, as much as we value our similarities. We each bring out unique selves, as we work together toward a common goal of being our best selves, both individually and collectively. Seeing the best in each other and talking about it publicly helps others (and ourselves) recognize our potential. Recognizing our commonalities—we are all human, we all breathe the same air, we are all mortal, we all have hopes and dreams—emphasizes our similarities despite differences, whether it's a style of play, a way of thinking, race, lifestyle."

Subsequently, when I asked Cindy Timchal about her take on *compassion*, she summarized it all in the following sentence: "Loving each other."

In the Win the Day culture of Way of Champions, I always emphasize the importance of self-compassion as well. Far too many individuals forget the value of this concept, and I try to make sure we all understand what it's about.

Are you constantly judging yourself, comparing yourself to others, holding yourself to unreasonable standards or to other people's expectations? Are you beating yourself up, putting yourself down, or limiting your peace and happiness by limiting your self-love? We must practice compassion. *Compassion*—both for the self and for others—is an immensely powerful and peace-loving tool. This state of mind alters brain frequencies, affecting neurophysiology, and thus causes physical states to be more relaxed, yet robust and energetic.

Often, we find space to be understanding and patient with others but we turn inward and treat ourselves more harshly. On the contrary, hold yourself lightly. Think of yourself—the individual, the being—quietly for a moment, and conscientiously relax your face. Feel love, patience, and care for the deepest parts of you, even if in the face of any other feelings, you may discover, while down there. Tell yourself: "It's okay. I'm taking things slow, and that's just fine. I'm perfect, just the way I am." You are not your possessions or your relationship status or your career or your bank account. At our core, we are all just BEINGS, and you must find a way to accept yourself on the BEING level.

This pronouncement does not mean that you lose ambition to strive for goals and greater expression of your life. It does not mean, however, that you let go of your principles to live in high moral-character. On the other hand, if occasionally you slip up … No problem! We're

red mango/Shutterstock.com

At our core, we are all just BEINGS, and you must find a way to accept yourself on the BEING level.

all human, we make mistakes, and we learn from them. If we're not in the place that we want to be, but we know that we could be, that's okay! What's the rush? We have long lives to live and love and accomplish; we are just where we're supposed to be right now.

So, hold yourself a bit more lightly. Your life is indeed an important and meaningful matter, but that doesn't mean you must take is so seriously all the time. Smile to yourself, right now. Laugh, in fact, at the silliness of being so serious. We're here to have fun and to love—both ourselves and others. To love requires patient understanding, as well as easy, unconditional care—indeed, true *compassion*. You deserve patience and care; you are worthy of being loved. Remember, there's only one *you* in this world. Cherish and honor that unique being.

Suzanne Tucker/Shutterstock.com

To love requires patient understanding, as well as easy, unconditional care—indeed, true compassion.

Finally, I would like to close with the astute observations of Coach Steve Kerr. When I asked him about *compassion*, he admitted it was an important aspect of his team's culture—winning and losing together. In the end, the player's nationality, language, tastes in music, or religious beliefs are not sources of division, but rather are, in fact, mediums for greater friendships, understanding, and success. These brilliant words resonate with the Chinese symbol for *compassion*, which depicts a generosity of the heart, followed by an active eagerness to participate in the opponent's joy or sorrow. This mindset is how caring and connection create successful cultures. The Kerr-era Warriors certainly could be defined in this ancient way for modern times.

COMMITMENT:
Devotion to a Worthy Cause

There are only two options regarding commitment.
You're either IN or OUT.

—Pat Riley, President of the Miami Heat; Former NBA Coach

There are several factors you may wish to entertain as being worthy commitments in sport's cultures. As such, the following can be given some serious consideration.

Implementation

Athletes who display deep desire and discipline have a strong *commitment* to succeed. It's a characteristic that distinguishes great athletes from good ones. All factors considered, when a person is committed, the sky's the limit.

Commitment, on the other hand, doesn't have a life of its own. It will begin to fade, if it's not nurtured and fed. As a coach, your plans, objectives, and goals can motivate your athletes to persevere, until results are achieved. These goals must either be attainable, or frustration and disappointment will quickly set in. They must also be challenging, or boredom and burnout will result.

To measure an athlete's level of *commitment*, ask, "What three things are you willing to do in practice each day (or in each competition) to prove to yourself that you are serious about your *commitment* to the team, the coach, and your own personal improvement in this sport?" Over the years, I have heard a variety of answers, such as "give verbal support to teammates," "help the coaches with equipment care, distribution, and collection after practice," "sprint on defense, go for the 50/50 ball."

Once these answers are specified, the athlete can write affirmations about them on index cards. I ask the athletes to share their "big three" with their teammates, a process which makes them more accountable to everyone. These smaller *commitments* can be upgraded or replaced weekly, as an athlete begins to approach the bigger goals, the greater overall picture.

To further demonstrate their intent, have athletes create a contract and sign it, as an outward expression of their *commitment*. Copies can be made and distributed to their teammates. In addition, coaches can keep a copy on file. Draw up a contract for individual athletes that centers on a team objective or plan.

This exercise creates the opportunity for athletes to be responsible and accountable for their *commitments*. Monitor the athletes' responses to be sure that they are challenging, expansive, and aligned with your mission for the team. By having frequent (weekly or every other week) team meetings

Chalermpon Poungpeth/Shutterstock.com

In athletics, as well as other aspects of your life, your level of commitment is constantly being tested.

on the subject, you can talk with individual athletes, provide feedback, and work with them to adjust their choices.

This scenario is simply an opportunity to teach, as well as to guide and support their choices. Listen to athletes' observations and comments about their progress. Invite them to change or revise their big three, especially after they've had the chance to view their teammates' *commitments*. When an athlete seems to be down or performing poorly, remind them to think about the contract and what can be done to get back on track.

In athletics, as well as other aspects of your life, your level of *commitment* is constantly being tested. A variety of the more easily recognizable indicators that you have made a commitment to a certain path exists, including the following: you insist that you will not make excuses for marginal performance; you view your competitor as a partner to help bring out your best; you thirst for new ways to improve; you are eager to put forth extra effort, when needed; you experience an absence of lingering doubt; you refuse to view discouragement and disappointment as anything but natural; and you feel a natural and all-encompassing sense of joy and motivation to do all you can to be the best you can be.

The sky is the limit, when you demonstrate a consistent, never-ending *commitment* to what you deeply desire and want to achieve. It is the main ingredient that separates ordinary performers from those individuals who do extraordinary things. True *commitment* is devotion to a cause, an ideal, or a goal that may be more crucial than victory itself. The value of commitment is reflected in the following quotation:

Until one is committed, there is hesitancy; the chance to draw back...there is one elementary truth, the ignorance of which kills countless ideas and splendid plans: that the moment one commits oneself, then providence moves too. All sorts of things occur to help one that never would have occurred ... unforeseen incidents, meetings, and material assistance, which no man [or woman] could have dreamed, would come his way.

—Johann Wolfgang von Goethe,
German poet and philosopher

Consider whether your lack of *commitment* is simple complacency or whether you might want to look deeper to see if there is another sport or activity that will engender a higher level of *commitment.* In other words, a lack of *commitment* may be a sign that it's time to move on to something else that's more appropriate to your development at this particular moment in your life. Remember, too, that if your performance consistently falls short of your potential, you may lack *commitment.* Anything that is truly important to you in life is worthy of your full *commitment.*

Whatever you can do or dream you can, begin it.
Boldness has genius, power, and magic in it.
Begin it now.

—Johann Wolfgang von Goethe,
German Writer and Statesman

COURAGEOUSNESS:
Show Up, Dare Greatly

People say to me all the time 'you have NO fear.' I tell them, 'no, that's not true. I'm scared all the time. You have to have fear in order to have courage. I'm a courageous person, because I'm a scared person.'

—Ronda Rousey, American Professional Wrestler and Mixed Martial Artist Performer

In the words of author Ray Bradbury, "*First you jump off the cliff and build your wings on the way down.*" It takes courage to jump and trust that you'll build your wings on the way down. Most people stand at the top waiting endlessly for the wings to be built, before they jump. The point being discussed is about the *courage* to take that plunge, a risk few individuals are willing to take. Although those individuals who do risk are fearful, they go anyway. It's like the story of the young boy in Brazilian author Paulo Coelho's *The Alchemist*, who takes the trek across a vast desert, trusting that there will be a caravan coming in his direction that will have the supplies he needs to complete the journey.

Life is filled with stories of heroes, risk-takers, and warriors of indomitable spirit, who take the chance they are given to realize something greater than they can imagine. This mindset is what a Win the Day champion does. A champion has heart. The word *courage* in French is Coeur, and in Spanish, it is corazon, both when translated mean heart.

It is said that when racing horses die, only the champion receives a burial ceremony. They discard the body and bury the head and the heart—the two parts of anatomy that enabled the horse to never give up, competing all-out, even in pain. Like horses, champion athletes compete with heart, having the *courage* to give their all.

When I think of *courage*, I always remember the brilliant words spoken by Theodore Roosevelt in his speech, "The Man in the Arena" in 1910:

> *It is not the critic who counts; not the man who points out how the strong man stumbles, or where the doer of deeds could have done them better. The credit belongs to the man who is actually in the arena, whose face is marred by dust and sweat and blood; who strives valiantly; who errs, who comes short again and again, because there is not effort without error and shortcoming; but who does actually strive to do the deeds; who knows great enthusiasms, the great devotions; who spends himself in a worthy cause; who at best knows in the end the triumph of high achievement, and who at the worst, if he fails, at least fails while daring greatly, so that his place shall never be with those cold and timid souls who neither know victory nor defeat.*

Win the Day culture athletes and coaches are not timid souls. They are not afraid of failure, knowing that loss and setbacks are great teachers. They may fail, but do so "daring greatly." They then get back up and try it again, wiser and stronger. They show up, which is half the battle. Many individuals in this world never show up. In championship cultures, everyone is "all-in," living the core values and engaging with being authentic and vulnerable. Without question, that's what could be called awesome *courage*.

In Brené Brown's book, *Daring Greatly*, a title taken from Theodore Roosevelt's aforementioned speech, she talks about this great *courage*. "We must walk into the arena, whatever it may be … with *courage*. We must dare to show up and let ourselves be seen." Too many athletes hold back, fearful of going all out, because they may look silly; fail; let their team, coach, or parents down; make a mistake; or not be good enough. A true champion, as I have learned over the years, is willing to dare greatly, jump off the cliff, knowing that others will "have their back." That's the Win the Day attitude.

sirtravelalot/Shutterstock.com

A true champion is willing to dare greatly, jump off the cliff, knowing that others will "have their back."

There's an ancient expression that basically says the arrow that hits the bullseye is the result of 100 misses. Ultimately, after many attempts, it finds the target. This situation happens all the time with my work. Sometimes,

I make 100 calls to get one positive "yes." I've had numerous rejections with my attempts to publish books, yet have wound up with some bestsellers. I've lost more competitive events than I've won, but courageously came back for more, as a wiser competitor.

The University of Maryland women's field hockey team had just beaten Old Dominion University 3-2 in overtime, gaining a slot in the Final Four in Boston. My work with the Maryland team throughout the year consistently emphasized the need for athletes to play with their hearts (*courage*) and the importance of the team over the individual. In reality, this tactic is always a challenge with a team with many stars.

Following their victory, the Maryland Terps received the highest of compliments and greatest validation for their efforts. the Old Dominion coach said, "Maryland competed, hustled, and played with their hearts. When a team does that, it is very difficult to beat. Maryland won as a team."

What did the Old Dominion coach mean by the statement, "They played with their hearts?" Arguably, *heart* can be defined as the willingness to take risks to improve, even in the face of potential failure; the *courage* to go all-out and discover your capability at the moment; the freedom to lose, learn from it, and forge ahead; and planning with fearlessness, tenacity, and the audacity of being bold, as you look at your opponents and dare them to match your intensity.

For champions, this mentality is the spirit of play. Athletes playing only with their heads tend to be too ego-involved, smitten with themselves, and overly concerned with outcomes and winning. Courageous athletes and

Aspen Photo/Shutterstock.com

A coach helps a team cultivate courage by giving the athletes the freedom to fail.

coaches, on the other hand, have a deep desire to win. On the other hand, if they don't win, they refuse to measure their self-worth by any outcome. According to American Olympian gymnast, Simone Biles, "being a gymnast means having the strength to hold on and the courage to let go." As such, letting go and moving on from defeat is a courageous action.

Implementation

So, how do you coach the value of courageousness in your Win the Day culture? A coach helps a team cultivate *courage* by giving the athletes the freedom to fail. As a result, these athletes learn, therefore, that mistakes and setbacks are necessary components of the improvement process. Learning from these failures helps them to develop the most challenging, difficult athletic skills. If you do not have the freedom to let go of failure, you take no risks. As a consequence, you come to a full stop on the road to greatness (see the segment on the value of fearlessness).

When your athletes fail, suggest that they step back, embrace the failure, and learn from it. Athletes should know that you see failure in this way. In this setting, courage is what you expect. Then, when failure of any kind occurs, take the time (immediately at practice, perhaps the next day, if it occurs in a game) to ask the athlete, "What did you learn from that situation? What could you do to prevent such mistakes in the future?"

Rather than fighting their failures, athletes gain from seeing them as a natural experience that must occur. When they feel most devastated from taking a risk and suffering a setback, they can be reassured that they are about to learn from the experience in some way that will help them improve. If they overlook this lesson or resist learning from it, they will create new limitations that will impede their performance.

Specifically, ask your athletes to demonstrate *courage* by accepting embarrassment when it comes. For example, this factor may entail diving for control of a loose ball or coming back after taking a hard fall. It may mean holding their heads high, when losing a game, if they went all-out. It may involve taking the open shot, after having already missed five in a row, facing the crowd on the opponent's home court, and doing the right thing in all situations.

Next, you can set the stage for success by encouraging your athletes to take risks. Risk-taking can be fulfilling, exhilarating, and rewarding. The following "*courage* to risk" formula is an effective way that Bob Hansen has used successfully with all of his 15 Middlebury College men's championship tennis teams:

- He tells them that according to philosopher and French author André Gide, "Man cannot discover new oceans, unless he has the courage to lose sight of the shore." *Courage* indicates a willingness to take risks.

- If you take the risk and experience a setback, you should ask yourselves to think of the impact that this setback will have on your life in five years. This context helps put it into perspective. In most cases, you'll see that the setback is meaningless, aside from the wonderful lessons it can teach.
- When you take the time to choose realistic, short-term, challenging goals, you minimize the risk factors. When you select a direction of personal passion, you fortify your courage to take the risk.
- Bob then explains that the pain of taking a risk must be weighed against the pain of not taking the risk, which could be a life of deep regret or remorse. "Although I initially resist taking big risks, I usually end up taking them for their hidden opportunities. For the most part, my life can be seen as a series of constant, well-calculated risks. These thoughts and strategies help me go for it."

I love the way Bob self-discloses his personal life to his athletes during a teachable moment. This way of speaking shows his courage to be vulnerable (see the segment on value vulnerability).

Remember that success is already yours for having the *courage* to take the risk. After all, the most damaging or painful risk could very well be *not* taking the risk to improve your life. Don't ask, "Will this risk create failure?" Better to ask, "Will this risk put me in position for major breakthroughs and growth?" The only real failure is the un-fulfillment or remorse created by avoiding taking risks.

There's no comparison between what's lost by not trying and what's lost by not succeeding.

—Francis Bacon, English Philosopher and Statesman

GRATEFULNESS:
Finding Deep Meaning

Gratefulness is the key to a happy life that we hold in our hands, because if we are not grateful, then no matter how much we have, we will not be happy—because we will always want to have something else or something more.

—David Steindl-Rast, Catholic Benedictine Monk

Brother David, as he is affectionately known to his friends and followers, is a world-renowned Benedictine monk, most associated with the sacred value of *gratefulness*. (Go to gratefulness.org to learn more about this amazing man.) Over the course of several years, I've been blessed to get to know Brother David during several personal, intimate lunch meetings, as well as walks, at the Esalen Institute on the California Big Sur coast.

During one of my most difficult, challenging, and frightening times in my life, worried about the potential loss of one of my children, he taught me the value of gratefulness for what I did have, an opportunity to have four full years of love with this beautiful child, my first son, Daniel. We prayed and meditated together for Danny, and Brother David helped me to refocus on getting close, rather than to pull away. By so doing, the pain of potential loss faded into the background. I'm happy to tell you that Daniel is very much alive and super healthy today, at the age of 35. In fact, he ran for 35 kilometers on his 35th birthday. As such, *gratefulness* changed my life, and it continues to help me influence those individuals whom I'm so fortunate to have in my life … like you.

I'm tempted to fill up the rest of this section of the book with inspiring quotes from Brother David … and that may be more useful than what I have to say, but you can google Brother David and be exposed to all of his profound wisdom. Meanwhile, let me show you how I can help you and your culture to marinate in the "holy water" of gratitude.

Implementation

Let's be honest with ourselves, as coaches and athletes, we are very blessed to be working at something we love to do. Most individuals go to an office and work in a cubicle; we get to play a game. Being aware of this factor begins deep within our hearts, our source of gratitude.

Being grateful contributes to your overall health and well-being, builds strong relationships and cultures, and has a profound impact on positive performance. In fact, I use the term "from grateful to great." Having experienced over a hundred championship teams and thousands of champion athletes, I can anecdotally assure you that a culture of shared gratitude promotes a stronger team, as well as heightened levels of productivity and improved performance.

When your team arrives for practice or at the competitive arena, chances are their minds are full and their hearts empty. In reality, in all likelihood, there is much distraction from trivial, unimportant nonsense or heavy-weighing issues that detract from the present moment. The coaches with whom I work love the focus on a team having gratefulness, which brings them back to the task of winning the day, being present in the moment, and being mindful of why they do what they do.

The following exercise is one way to implement the habit of *gratefulness* in your championship culture: Before you begin your workout, training session, or work for the day, you need to think of seven aspects of life that you appreciate, for example, your skills, talents, mind, health, family, friends, opportunities, and work. Next, with your eyes closed, you need to connect to the feeling of appreciation. Give yourself a minute to get this feeling. Then, "Imagine this feeling coming into your body in three deep breaths, as each breath surrounds the heart. Hold each breath there, as the feeling begins to expand." With this sensation of gratitude in your heart, make your performance today a reflection and extension of that appreciation. Finally, open your eyes and take on the day's tasks. Feel your vitality and positive attitude about bringing your best to the challenges you face.

Monkey Business Images/Shutterstock.com

Being grateful contributes to your overall health and well-being, builds strong relationships and cultures, and has a profound impact on positive performance.

When I introduced this exercise to Middlebury College men's tennis coach Bob Hansen decades ago, he began to use it on a regular basis prior to practice. In fact, he did this exercise the morning of his most recent national championship in 2018.

Another *gratefulness* exercise that I use in my coaching is to have the team sit in a circle and ask them to tell the teammate to their left why they are grateful about them as a person, as well as a significant athlete on the team. The room becomes inundated with love, as the bond between them gets even stronger. This exercise works especially well prior to a big tournament or at another significant time during the season.

Finally, I love to write a daily email of gratitude to a friend, colleague, or athlete to help set a positive tone not only for them, but for myself as well. When you give love, you get it back a hundred times (see the segment on the power of love). When I do this, I feel more optimistic, more alive, and better about my life. It has been scientifically shown that such *gratefulness* increases the activity in the brain's pleasure centers. In fact, who of us does not enjoy pleasure?

I've been teaching the value of *gratefulness* in my cultures for decades. I believe it's what separates my Way of Champions, Win the Day cultures from others. When you decide to coach the aforementioned *gratefulness* exercises, not only will your athletes love them, the "joy factor" will rise exponentially (see the segment on the value of joy). Speaking of joy, I will close this section with another piece of Brother David's wisdom:

As we learn to give thanks for all of life and death, for all of this given world of ours, we find deep joy. It is the joy of trust, the joy of faith in the faithfulness at the heart of all things. It is the joy of gratefulness in touch with the fullness of life.

INTEGRITY: Search for Uncompromising Principles

Integrity is life's search for uncompromising principles, a voyage to find yourself and demonstrate that in an authentic way.

—Pete Carroll, Head Coach, Seattle Seahawks

I am in awe of the dynamic, universal relevance of the value of *integrity* and how many other values are related to and subsumed under its umbrella. When I think about *integrity*, I must also consider the all-inclusive aspects of values such as authenticity, accountability, resilience, humility, gratefulness, vulnerability, and character. In this sense *integrity* becomes the mother of many values, demonstrated in numerous ways. I can also attest to the fact that most coaches I meet while sharing my work agree how *integrity* is manifested in so many ways within their cultures. In the words of American author and theorist Buckminster Fuller, "*integrity* is the essence of everything successful."

Anson Dorrance, head women's soccer coach at the University of North Carolina told me recently that in his culture, "we have verbal leaders who are less concerned about popularity than they are about holding everyone to their highest standards while driving teammates to their potential. This is accountability and *integrity*. We demand that everyone get on board with this."

Bob Hansen, head men's tennis coach at Middlebury College, told me the story about how his team was gracious to one of their opponents after having been beaten by them twice in the season, once being in the championship match. This display of *integrity* with character and authenticity paid off the following year, when the results were reversed, and their opponent was gracious to them in defeat.

Implementation

Cindy Timchal, head women's lacrosse coach at the United States Naval Academy, believes that her teams demonstrate *integrity* when they, as she says it, "narrow the gap between what we say we'll do and what we actually do." Her team makes promises to each other (see section on Win the Game or Win the Day) and then follows through with *integrity*, delivering the "goods."

Phil Jackson notices how *integrity* plays out, when his team focused their hearts and souls on something greater than themselves, something you never forget.

Then, there is the late coach Bill Walsh, former head coach of the NFL San Francisco Forty-Niners, five-time Super Bowl champs. Rather than focus on winning championships, he devoted his energy to developing a strong culture of *integrity*. His standards are noteworthy, and every coach should implement each one into their culture. These standards can easily be posted as daily reminders, when your team shows up. They can also be used in team meetings, as well as coaching talking points on the field. His six standards for coaches were as follows:

- Develop respect for each other regardless of your role (see the segment on the value of being respectful).
- Be firm and be fair.
- Give positive praise (see the section on positivity).
- Focus on effort, not results (see the segment on the value of grit).

- Have open communications (see the segment on the value of listening).
- Everyone gives to the team (see the segment on the value on selflessness).

The late coaching icon, Dean Smith, head men's basketball coach at the University of North Carolina for several decades, thought about *integrity*, making it part of his three core values. In my one-and-only meeting with Coach Smith, a few years before he passed, he related to me how he wanted every player to feel like they were the most important athlete who ever played for him. I can tell you this, after that 45 minutes meeting with him, I felt like I was the most important person in his life. Imagine how inspiring that was. Subsequently, I began to write my bestselling book, *Coaching With Heart*, a week after this fortuitous meeting. He did mention to me how we need to place people above all else, how the team is more important than the individual, and the significance of personal *integrity*. In reality, all three items were the special values of a championship culture. This naturally marinated my spirit in the RIVER effect (see that segment in Part II).

The Chinese symbols for *integrity* illustrate wholeness of character and a commitment to stand up for personal principles—never for a moment, considering compromising what you believe to be right. Buddhist thought asks that you do the right thing, act with *integrity* in all things. For all coaches, *integrity* is the act of narrowing the existential gap between what you say or feel and what you do.

Athletics presents you with continual opportunities to demonstrate your *integrity*. You may say you train hard, and yet when others are not looking, you back off of the intensity. You may say you'll show up, but don't. You might claim you want to get in shape, yet indulge in counterproductive eating habits. There are many ways this gap between what you say and what you do can manifest.

There is another way you can compromise your *integrity* that happens frequently in sports: not playing to your full potential. *Integrity* is the refusal to compromise your talents, regardless of the score, the outcome, or the differences in levels of ability among competitors. Do not give others permission to make you feel inferior, undeserving, or less than you are.

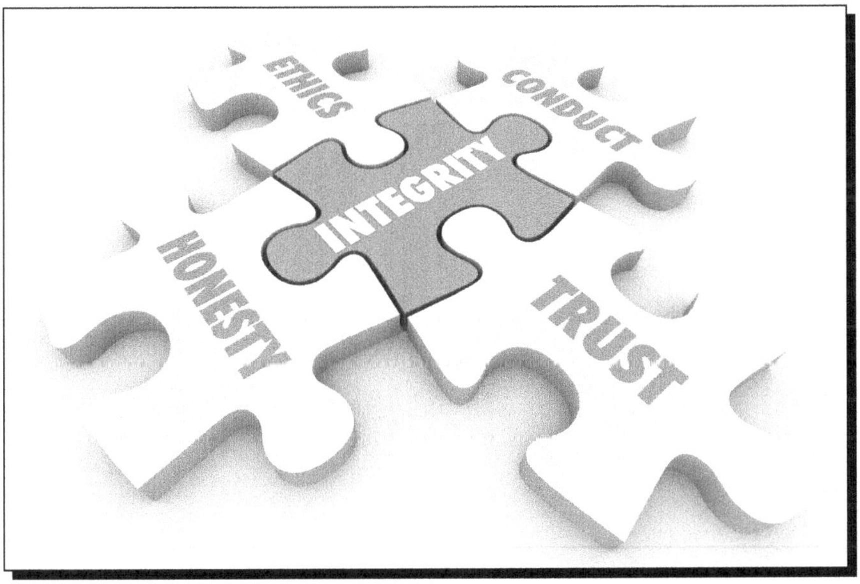

iQoncept/Shutterstock.com

For all coaches, integrity is the act of narrowing the existential gap between what you say or feel and what you do.

I tell the athletes and coaches in my cultures that we must identify and cultivate deep-rooted values. I've done this with you in this book. There are multiple ways to implement all of them into your Win the Day culture.

Integrity is the refusal to "sell out" on these values and on your true self.

> *Hold to your ethics and principles and do not compromise what you believe to be right.*
>
> *Acting in concert with your dreams and visions, being honest with yourself and in harmony with the laws of nature are the keys to having integrity.*
>
> —*I Ching #29*

JOYFULNESS: Raising the Fun Factor

One of the reasons they are so special is they have so much joy in the process of each game. They don't talk much about records. But our guys have a lot of fun from one night to the next. I think that's part of our success. It comes from enjoying everything every day.

—Steve Kerr, Head Coach, Golden State Warriors

To be perfectly honest, I could fill this part of the book on joy with conversations, emails, and texts I've had with Coach Kerr over the past four years and all I've learned from him about being a champion coach. He's extended to me the opportunity to contribute my expertise, but I believe I've learned and benefitted more from this relationship than he has. My point is, our "consultancy" is filled with joy and fun, as we continue to love what this endeavor is truly about, making a difference in each other's lives. Because of our relationship, I can now fully understand why he's such an awesome coach and why his guys go the distance under his tutelage.

Let's talk more about this. The first and most important of the Warriors' core values is joy! Steve wants everyone to have fun. It's a game, and individuals play because of the fun-factor. It's fun to be a Warrior, because they are a selfless brotherhood of athletes, coming together for each other for something bigger than the game. With this environment, everyone feels safe. As a result, they love playing with each other. When you have fun, you will work harder and have greater commitment and motivation to compete.

From a fan's perspective, the Warriors are fun to watch, as are the fans. I love being at the games not just to watch a great culture of athletes, but to watch a fun-loving fan base, celebrating joy and excitement. I can easily absorb the *joy* the bench players are having, when a teammate, starter, or sub, does something special. The guys literally "jump for *joy*." It is fun knowing that all of your teammates want the best for you. While selflessness (see the segment on the value of selflessness) is truly noble, they buy in because of the joyful results they get from giving to each other. It's fun and joyful to be part of an organization that allows its athletes the bandwidth to be themselves in all its diverse population. It's joyful to be part of a loving, caring coaching staff that actually listens to you. When Steve first took over as coach, his idea was to find ways his guys could be happy (see the section on don't worry, be happy). Happiness translates into joyfulness. It is because of this happiness that, for a large part, his team is successful.

What I want you to take away from this is how *joy* and selflessness can play a key role in your culture, as well by implementing the aforementioned philosophy of Steve Kerr, why and how his team experiences *joy*.

Implementation

The culture of Bob Hansen, Middlebury College head men's tennis coach, is also built on *joy* for many of the same reasons as the Warriors. Being Warrior fans, Bob and I have discussed the element of *joy* and how he has instituted the Kerr culture of *joy* into his team environment. Simply put: Sports is *joy*. The promise his team makes to each other every season is that they will have more fun and *joy* than any other team, anywhere. I asked Bob, "more than the Warriors?" Now, that's a challenge. Bob's team has even gone so far as to imitate the inclusion of music into their practice sessions, as do the Warriors.

Phil Jackson talks about truly coming from being truly present in each and every moment, not just when things are going your way. Of course, things go your way when you stop worrying about whether you'll win or lose and focus your full attention on the *joy* that's happening in the moment, the fun of trying to execute a well-designed plan.

Missy Foote, former head women's lacrosse coach at Middlebury College, has some wonderful insight into the value of *joy* and how she implemented *joy* into her team's culture. According to Missy, "belly laughs, celebrations, and traditions inherently create *joy* on teams, but I think the coach is crucial in helping set the tone for how to

Jacob Lund/Shutterstock.com

Sports is joy.

have fun, not take life too seriously, and how to recognize *joy* in small accomplishments." The following is how she specifically established fun and *joy* with her teams:

- After hard sprints or conditioning, I like to remind my players that hard experiences, when shared, are joyful and life-affirming. "We don't do sprints (only) for the conditioning," I like to say.
- The last words I always say to my team in the huddle before a game are, "Have fun out there!" I wanted those words to imprint on their minds to ward off becoming bogged down in game plan details, as they headed out to the field. Championship athletes play with *joy*, fortitude, fierceness, and adaptability.
- I've often stopped practice to point out the backdrop of purple mountains, as the sun sets, featuring crazy cloud formations, a dandelion covered meadow, or geese flying overhead. Experiencing *joy* as a sense of wonder in the everyday helps everyone put into perspective their shared experiences and can help promote a feeling of loving kindness.

I love Missy's approach to creating *joy* in the moment. As such, I encourage you and your athletes to take a few moments to notice the beauty all around: the colors, the ball, its texture on the surface, the court, field, pool, track. Simply feeling grateful for this moment, in which everyone is alive and healthy gives the opportunity to experience the subtle, quiet joy of being together. Whether it's conditioning or skill development, look for ways to bring more *joy* to the equation. Coaches who have well-disciplined teams realize that athletes will be more receptive to hard work, if there's some fun involved; they will go the extra mile if they enjoy what they do.

WoodysPhotos/Shutterstock.com

Fun doesn't mean you take the job of training less seriously.

It's important not to confuse fun with goofing off. Cindy Timchal, while she was the head women's lacrosse coach at the University of Maryland, often talked to her players about the fun in the execution of a well-thought-out offensive plan.

Sir Roger Bannister, the first athlete to run a sub-four-minute mile, talked about the *joy* and fun of going all out, even while experiencing pain. Fun doesn't mean you take the job of training less seriously. Fun is simply toning down the stress, anxiety, and pressure. In fact, fun is why most athletes started engaging in their sport in the first place!

Find drills or workouts that your athletes can do well, which will be fun for them, especially if you can end a practice with them. On occasion, it can be fun for athletes to decide that they'd like to do that last 20 minutes of practice. An unstructured, unsupervised scrimmage also works well for many game sports. In that regard, some of the great lacrosse coaches have their teams play soccer at practice every so often. Some soccer coaches play touch football; some football coaches conduct box-ball games. The possibilities for fun are unlimited—the key point is to just have fun!

RESPECTFUL:
Creating a Spirit of Loyalty

Respect of others creates a spirit of loyalty.

Followers are motivated to take on hardship and sacrifice in the attainment of goals.

—*I Ching, the Chinese Book of Changes*

In the culture of North Carolina's women's soccer, head coach Anson Dorrance, in a recent phone conversation, mentioned how "we don't whine or create drama out of *respect* for each other. We don't freak out over silly issues or reside in tenuous states of emotional catharsis." These athletes *respect* each other for competing hard in practice against each other. They *respect* the game, the officials, and the opponent.

Of course, you can't legislate *respect*, but as a coach, you can walk your talk and model what you want to see in your athletes. This value begins with each of us respecting ourselves. We begin to *respect* ourselves, when we uphold our core values, like commitment, character, positivity, selflessness, and integrity. When you have all these, you'll begin to *respect* yourself, which will bleed over into your *respect* for others.

To build *respect* in your culture, think about using the RIVER effect, the Relationship Game, the Power of Influence and the segment on feelings from Part II, and the impact that these have on building *respect*. Staying true to all your culture's values also strengthens the *respect* others have for you. The coach sets the tone for a community that demonstrates *respect*.

Great coaches and leaders, such as former Chicago Bulls' head coach Phil Jackson, created environments that were trusting, open, and respectful. Jackson understood that he gained power by having *respect* for his athletes. They then mirrored his behavior, as they achieved high levels of performance. In your other roles in life, such as that of a CEO or a parent, you may have also discovered how *respect* helps create the outcome you desire.

When I asked Pete Carroll, head coach of the Seattle Seahawks, about the value of *respect*, he reminded me that his team's culture is guided by values of acceptance of diversity, which is rooted in the notion of *respect*, as they practice inclusivity on and off the field. In fact, there is *respect* for a wide range of human differences within the Seattle Seahawk culture.

Legendary UCLA basketball coach John Wooden claimed that *respect* starts with giving *respect* to others. "You

oneinchpunch/Shutterstock.com

Respect starts with giving respect to others.

must have *respect* for those under your supervision. Then, they will do what you ask...go the extra distance, make the extra effort in trying to accomplish the most they can."

An attitude of *respect* is a crucial factor in achieving high-levels of performance. Personally, I know of a collegiate women's basketball team that was talented, passionate, and united as a group, yet could never realize its potential and win, because the coaching staff was blatantly disrespectful and abusive, to each other, as well as to the athletes. Sarcasm, shame, and foul language tore these great spirits apart, and their performance reflected this hostile environment. Healthy coach-athlete relationships are built on trust and loyalty, through positive communication and forgiveness. The key is to *respect* all others, as you would like to be respected.

Think of throwing a stone in the center of a pond and how every ripple reaching outward begins at the single point at which the stone was initially dropped. In the same way, all *respect* for others initially begins with *self-respect*. In Chinese, the symbols for *respect* express the understanding that *respect* for others begins with *respect* for yourself. With such *respect*, you create an environment that is conducive to extraordinary performance. *Respect* is one aspect of love, and when an athlete feels respected and loved by a coach, they will go the distance—do what is asked and more. When you *respect* and love others, you don't lose power or control; you gain it. A lack of *respect* creates resistance, alienation, and resentment—even revolt.

Implementation

If you wish to implement the core value of *respect* in your culture, answer these questions: What do you need to *start doing* that you're currently not doing in order to create a more respectful culture? What do you need to *stop doing* that you are presently doing in order to create a more respectful culture? Make the answers a new set of promises you make to Win the Day.

SELFLESSNESS: It's About Pointing Fingers

One player's selfish attitude can poison a locker room and make it hard, if not impossible, to establish team work. Basketball is a team game about unselfish acts and sacrifice that result in team building.

—Dean Smith, Head Men's Basketball Coach, University of North Carolina

I love the ancient Kenyan proverb: "sticks in a bundle are unbreakable." The spirit of a solid team culture never breaks, when its members stick together, unselfishly, helping everyone on the team reach higher levels of performance. When you do this, you collectively Win the Day.

Bill Bradley, senator, author, all-American and professional basketball player with the New York Knicks, comments, "The greatness of my teams is how they realized that no one player could be as good as all of the players competing together unselfishly."

The aforementioned quote by Dean Smith to introduce the core value of *selflessness* was part of a conversation we had, while I was working at UNC. He taught me and his players that such a value helps to bring out their best. It was Coach Smith who promoted the "pointing finger," a gesture made by pointing to the teammate who assisted you on scoring a basket as a way to share the effort. This action was part of what he called "The Carolina Way," a way of caring and connecting to Win the Day.

Such a culture becomes contagious. It was true at Carolina. As such, I experienced this value of *selflessness* with several of the Carolina coaches and teams during my seven-year tenure on the Tarheel's campus, such as women's volleyball, lacrosse, and soccer squads. For example, one of the main core values that Anson Dorrance, head women's UNC soccer coach, felt was basic to the culture of his teams, while willing 22-time national championships speaks to the concept of selfless behavior. The athletes buy into the premise that regardless of playing time, they remain noble and still support the team and its mission. "This self-sacrificing, generous human being always places team before self. We play for each other, helping all to be better."

It's not easy being selfless in today's world. Many cultures struggle with getting the athletes to "buy in" to the notion of *giving* rather than *getting*. As a coach, you need to consider being more demanding about this core value and teach your athletes how to embrace it more fully. Sustained *selflessness* becomes its own reward. When individuals give to others, others give back exponentially, which helps everyone to Win the Day.

Eleven-time national championship head coach Geno Auriemma of the University of Connecticut women's basketball team says that there is "too much of a 'me' culture in youth sports…it's all about me, me, me. Kids are influenced by pro athletes whom they see as being really cool. These athletes seem to always think about themselves." Auriemma's culture puts a high premium on *selflessness*, a code of behavior that he believes contributes so much to their success. This is a life skill that he expects his athletes to learn in order to promote caring and connection in their culture.

One of the stories I love to tell my teams is the one about Andre Iguodala of the Golden State Warriors. Evidently, when Steve Kerr took over as head coach with the Warrior's organization, one of his first acts was to talk with Andre about his role on the team. Andre, an NBA All-Star and consistent starter on every team he played for, every game of his career, was asked by Kerr how he'd feel if he didn't start with the Warriors and come off the bench, when needed, instead. Kerr told him how that would make the team better. Andre unselfishly responded that he would agree to do whatever is best for the team. He trusted Kerr, and contributed to his team in this way all season. Subsequently, Andre was called upon in the Finals of the 2015 Championship series to start, and his stellar performances earned him the MVP of those Finals, as the Warriors won their first championship with Steve Kerr. Arguably, all this happened, because Andre chose to selflessly Win the Day.

Because of the high priority Kerr puts on *selflessness*, his players find joy in giving to each other. Kerr states that the concept of *selflessness* is counterintuitive in professional sports, where many worry about getting enough—money, playing time, statistics, recognition, etc. Yet, Kerr finds a way to create a giving culture. His method is to ask players to be mindful of giving to each other as a way to ultimately get more in return. Notice how unselfishly they distribute the ball, throw an extra pass, and give credit to others for their contribution.

Of course, in Anson Dorrance's culture the athletes learn to put the team before self. Mia Hamm, a member of one of UNC's championship women's soccer teams, talks about the champion being the team, not any one individual player. I've observed Dorrance's teams in practice, and truthfully, they are a clan of generous people, who collectively place team above self.

Nancy Stevens, head coach of the University of Connecticut's women's field hockey national champions, shared her take on the value of *selflessness* with me, while working with her team. She started by quoting the following African proverb:

> *If you want to go fast, go alone. If you want to go far, go together.*

According to Stevens, "During the recruiting process, we often identify players who are supremely talented, but simply won't fit into our team culture. There is only one ball on the field! We look for players who enjoy sharing the ball. If you give up the ball, you will always get it back. The synergy created by playing as a team will often succeed

lz/Shutterstock.com

If you want to go fast, go alone. If you want to go far, go together.

against teams that depend on one of two superstar players. This philosophy has allowed us to win three of the past five NCAA National Championships.

"On a more personal note, I have had the good fortune to travel extensively in Africa over the past decade. Observing the strength of the tribe has inspired me to share aspects of those strong cultures with our team. I have also learned a great deal from observing herds of elephants. Dame Daphne Sheldrick who founded the Sheldrick Trust to rescue orphan elephants has said many times that, 'Elephants possess all the best qualities of human beings and very few of the worst.' I have observed the herd waiting for and protecting a younger elephant that limped slowly with a twisted leg. It was a congenital defect that prevented the younger elephant from keeping up with the herd. Rather than abandon the family member, different herd members took turns walking alongside this slower elephant. That is just one example of many that can be learned on the Masai Mara."

Implementation

As far as implementation of *selflessness* goes, you may want to try this. One of my favorite exercises to get teams to think more selflessly is to ask everyone to choose one way that they will give to the team this week, from a list of 10 items drawn up by the entire team. They then send a "group text," informing their teammates about their generosity for the week, and everyone keeps each other accountable for doing the work. Sometimes, it's about picking up all the balls, after practice, or carrying the ball bag, or giving more praise to others or volunteering to help other teammates with certain skill development. After a few weeks, the team begins to feel the shift, which creates a stronger bond between the players. The connection deepens, and the caring blossoms. They become givers, rather than getters.

I leave you with this thought from the Dalai Lama: "Our prime purpose in this life is to give to and help others." When you do, you Win the Day. We are on this planet to do one thing … serve.

There is a beautiful compelling story about *selflessness* told by Native American Lakota historian, Joseph Marshall III. He refers to *selflessness* as generosity, which is beautifully reflected in the following story:

"Early in the 19th century, a group of Lakota moving camp were forced to wait for an entire day. while a herd of buffalo, numbering in the hundreds of thousands, passed by. A young boy sat, somewhat impatiently, with his grandmother as they watched. 'Why are there so many?' he asked. The old woman smiled lovingly and replied, 'Because there is no end to the Earth's generosity. Do not let there be an end to yours.' " I love this fresh outlook that expresses the heart of the Lakota Nation toward *selflessness*, a wisdom that transcends the ages.

VULNERABILITY:
Leaning Into a Scary Place

Vulnerability is not weakness. And that myth is profoundly dangerous.

It's about showing up and being seen.

—Brené Brown, Ph.D., Researcher, and Author

Being *vulnerable* is a strength often related to being authentic. Great coaches are not afraid to be authentically *vulnerable* and admit they made a mistake or say "that loss is on me, I didn't prepare us well enough." Steve Kerr of the Golden State Warriors is such a coach. He'll apologize to players, if he keeps players on the bench too long. If a player has a disagreement with him about how he's being used, he listens and doesn't take it personally.

This trait is a value rarely found in the coaching profession or among athletes in all sports. We struggle with being authentic and *vulnerable*, because we think of it as weakness while in actuality it is strength. It demonstrates courage (see the segment on courageousness). In the words of Brené Brown, *daring greatly means the courage to be vulnerable.*

I know from a personal perspective how much courage it takes to be authentic and *vulnerable.* I've been practicing with these values in my coaching for 40 years. While I feel I'm only half way there, I keep experimenting with shedding my mask. My mission is not only to make a difference in the lives of others, it's to master my craft. Every year, I get closer to getting "mask-free, as well as emotionally "naked," on the never-ending journey toward full authenticity. It takes courage and the willingness to take risks to "show up and be seen" in the words of researcher/author Brené Brown.

I continue to work at being unapologetically me. It's a frightening place to visit, yet it is absolutely essential, if I hope to be effective and remain sensitive, caring, respectful, authentic, and genuine, so as to truly make a difference in the lives of others. It requires me to lean into this fearful, scary place and that takes courage … BUT, I can tell you that when I have the presence of heart to do this, it is so worth it.

Most people feel that in order to do their work well, they need a mask they can hide behind, such as a title, a degree, a rank, or a position. For me, however, I can't do my best work with a mask. I must put aside my author, athlete mask, come out from behind it, and meet you as

wavebreakmedia/Shutterstock.com

Great coaches are not afraid to be authentically vulnerable and admit they made a mistake.

a human being, in all my flaws and imperfections. This point is when I truly connect, heart-to-heart, rather than head-to-head. That's when the real work begins.

Those of you who know me and have attended any of my conferences and workshops know that I don't use the stage, microphone, or title. I dress comfortably and do not own a "power suit." I don't hide behind notes or a lectern. I'm being the same person I am, whether leading a group or swimming with my kids or talking with my friends. By being open and stripped of the entire "professional garb," as it were, I can be thoroughly seen and be someone, whom I would feel comfortable around. Why do I do this? I do this because I've learned that if I want to make a difference, I must connect and meet my audience, where they're at. I must be willing to look silly, make mistakes, forget what I said, fail, and even risk you not liking me.

My attitude is that we're all the same … human beings, not human doings ... who are here to help each other learn by sharing that part of ourselves. I need to learn from you what I need to know, so that I can help you to know what you need to learn. It's that simple.

I still get caught up into the "professional trap," and I can feel the distance between our hearts set in. I refuse to connect head-to-head, because no growth takes place. So, I try each time I get the opportunity to make a difference to show up and be seen—or, in my case, be experienced. The result of being authentic and *vulnerable* is that I gain the trust and respect of others, and they become loyal, secure, enthusiastic, and committed to "going the distance" with me. This situation demands "outside-the-box" behavior, out on the edge, fearlessly fighting to win the hearts of my athletes.

Allison Herreid/Shutterstock.com

As a human being, I need to learn from you what I need to know, so that I can help you to know what you need to learn.

Implementation

Such authenticity and vulnerability means you must trust yourself ... to be comfortable in your own skin ... to see all of your work as a path of humanity, and we all are humans just like those we lead and coach. Engage in conversation that unites, not separates. For example, draw an athlete in by asking: "So, what is your go-to comfort food?" Everyone relates to that. Food is the universal connector. You'll be pleasantly surprised to see where this opening takes the conversation. And, in the process, we all act human. I remember the Dalai Lama once telling an audience that he was just like us all ... same fears, concerns, troubles, desires. He was authentic, and from that place, he could lead me, and I would follow.

Whenever I am in a leadership role, I purposely remind myself to "let it all go and just BE ME." That is all I need to do to continue to be effective in that role. That's how I can connect more deeply and more authentically, and be *vulnerable*.

Being authentic and *vulnerable* for a coach is a subject that's slowly becoming part of the conversation in coaching education. Athletes are also realizing that being *vulnerable* is a good value. It means not being afraid to make a mistake, fail, mess up, or lose.

When that happens, when you're that authentic and *vulnerable*, fear flows away as you become free to fly, fluidly letting your body's innate intelligence take over. A free athlete is an awesome spectacle to watch. A free athlete has more fun and positions themselves for extraordinary performance. That's what I aspire to do when I'm working with large groups of people to discover their greatness.

Authenticity and *vulnerability* are liberating. They free everyone up to perform to their full capacity. More meaningfully, however, they enable everyone to experience more joy, fun, and love.

I recommend you watch, if you haven't already, The *Power of Vulnerability TED Talk* by the vulnerability champion, Brené Brown. This is the wave of the future for all sports performers and leaders—catch the wave now and ride it forever.

As previously noted, the following are two profound questions that can help you to implement the value of *vulnerability* and authenticity into your life, as a coach or athlete:

- What do you need to *start doing* that you're not currently doing in order to become more *vulnerable* and authentic in your work or life?

- What do you need to *stop doing* that you are presently doing in order to become more *vulnerable* and authentic in your work or life?

Vulnerability sounds like truth and feels like courage.

Truth and courage aren't always comfortable, but they're never weakness.

Vulnerability is the birthplace of everything we are hungry for.

—Brené Brown, Ph.D.

At this point, you are ready to venture into Part IV and carry your personal core values into the coaching arena to influence your team in the development of their cultural team values.

PART IV

ESTABLISHING TEAM VALUES—Win the Day Competing

The role of the head coach is to get his players to practice and demonstrate the culture's core values.

—Steve Kerr, Head Coach, Golden State Warriors

The Win the Day champion's journey is not unlike that of the sacred path of the combative warrior or the Native American vision quest. Such warriors were characterized by inner strength, mental toughness, and independence, and they fought for a higher good, beyond self-interest. They understood, as do champions, that the game is not only fought on the battlefield against an opponent; the game is also an arena for the battles within, against failure, fear, fatigue, frustration, self-doubt, and ego. They chose to fight these battles with "weapons of the heart." These weapons are their core values—competitive values that are more powerful than traditional weapons themselves.

The word *te* in Chinese means "virtue" or value, as in the *Tao Te Ching*, the classic book of the virtuous way. Being a Win the Day champion is a spiritual act of practicing these inner virtues of the heart. As such, this book is designed to help you to connect and demonstrate them in all arenas of athletics, and personal life.

Learning how to implement all of these timeless, team core values on a consistent basis will enable your culture to Win the Day. Furthermore, the point cannot be overemphasized that its implementation must be consistent. Coaching to the values on the practice field is essential. Catch your players "doing it right" and use it as an example for the entire team. When an athlete demonstrates a value, such as being fearless, blow the whistle, call the team together, and give praise where it's due. Point out how an athlete's work ethic is strong. Ask the group, "Who else thinks they can do that?"

This step keeps the culture honest and the athletes begin to understand how you want them to behave. You can facilitate this behavior shift by using highlight videos to point out how core values look, as well as help your athletes to recognize their effect on the overall culture. I also have my teams post the values in the locker room, keeping them visible. I also recommend that teams devote each week or month to a particular value and talk about it before each practice.

These values are rooted in the basic human needs of caring and connection. These core values are all factors that can be controlled. Although you can't control winning on the scoreboard, you can be more mindful and control winning the day, thereby positioning yourselves for good things to happen and having a say in the outcome. All the core values addressed in Part IV have been implemented in various ways by each of my championship teams, as well as the 12 iconic coaches noted throughout this book, to build successful sports cultures. As such, Part IV is designed to show you how to implement these core values in your team culture, not to win a championship, but to establish a way of being that could set the stage for achieving one.

According to Steve Kerr, "the role of the head coach is to get his players to practice and demonstrate the culture's core values." He believes what was noted previously—you must coach these values on the court. Steve also says that to get a team united and sacrifice for the team is difficult, which is why many coaches give up trying. He mentions that in order to accomplish this mindset, the whistle needs to be used as a core-value teaching moment, and that it must be done every day, consistently.

While all these core values sound great and noble, that's not enough. They must be operationalized for them to sink in. Notice the Warriors and what do you see? Their flow is in tune with each other. I know Steve and observe how the deeper core values of mindfulness, joy, compassion, and competitiveness are the essence of who he is and what he models. His players buy in to that model and play together for the greater good of the team.

You can do this, too. We all can. On the other hand, the message of Win the Day core values must be

Aspen Photo/Shutterstock.com

Although you can't control winning on the scoreboard, you can be more mindful and control winning the day, thereby positioning yourselves for good things to happen and having a say in the outcome.

reinforced in daily practice. Of course, Steve's biggest assets are his ability to respect all those individuals with whom he works, while controlling his ego, listening, and showing lots of love for his guys.

The remainder of Part IV features the 10 team core values, which represent those values of all my championship teams. As such, you are encouraged to employ your athletes' help identifying their own team values, either from the list presented in Part IV or from those standards of behavior they deem essential. This step helps to create a stronger "buy-in" by the players to the culture, as well as a way to take accountability and demonstrate ownership. Their list can either stand alone or be integrated into the several presented in Part IV.

The following is an example of how I recently did this exercise with two of my teams, the MLS pro team the San Jose Earthquakes and the Stanford University women's lacrosse squad. I divided them into three groups, by position and in a circle. They then chose one core value that they felt was relevant to the team. These were added to the core value deemed essential by the coach. What resulted was a bundle of four core values to be used by the entire team. Subsequently, they added an additional four values from the list I gave them for a total of eight core team values.

Feel free to experiment with this core value process and have fun creating your identity together—a set of values to guide how you play, compete, and live your lives together. They are what you stand for, side-by-side, no matter what the scoreboard tells you. They are the cultural essential absolutes, around which all decisions are made.

This is the perfect time to segue into Part IV, which will be comprised of 10 time-honored and time-tested team core values.

BELIEF: No Fixed Limits, No Fixed Mind

Dream BIG and believe, because dreams do come true.

To be an overachiever, you have to be an over believer.

—Dabo Swinney, Head Football Coach, Clemson University

As I sit here writing this book, I could be worried about the fact that I do not have a publisher yet and do not know how it will happen. Intuitively, however, I believe it will happen. That is belief, the faith I have in others recognizing the importance of this work and how it can make a substantial difference in the lives of others.

Belief in a culture is systemic. It begins, according to head coach Missy Meharg of the University of Maryland's women's field hockey team, with the understanding that "we are all in this together. We are family, and knowing that, makes it easier to believe in who we are, what we can do, and why we do it."

Head women's soccer coach at the University of North Carolina, Anson Dorrance, talking with me about competitive belief, says that with accomplishment comes confidence; and confidence leads to belief. It must be in that order.

On the other hand, what if you don't have 22 national championships on your list of accomplishments as Anson has? In USNA's head women's lacrosse coach Cindy Timchal's culture, "we act 'as-if' we're champions in practice, in games, in our meetings, and affirm strongly our belief that we are national champions. We haven't won one yet at the USNA but we have come close. In my second season of work with the 'middies,' we went to the final four, losing to Boston College by one goal in the semifinals. Navy wasn't even ranked in the top 20 pre-season. Continually affirming their greatness all season, coupled with our cultural core values and cultural wisdom, we 'went the distance'."

There is an expression I often use: what you believe, you receive. Everyone has, within themselves, all of what they need to accomplish extraordinary things. While the iconic bumblebee is too small, too heavy, and has a low aerodynamic structure, yet, it can fly hundreds of miles in a single day.

I love to tell my teams that their opponent's greatest advantage is your lack of belief in yourselves. I then proceed to mention that this belief they must have is not connected to outcomes or results. Their belief needs to focus on all that they can control—the little things, their promises, and their culture. I say you may or may not win the game, but you'll compete like crazy and play your very best. BELIEVE THAT!

Air Images/Shutterstock.com

What you believe, you receive.

Implementation

Coaching the value of *belief* with your culture is essential. For example, when you feel a sense of self-doubt and a lack of belief, know that you are probably concentrating too much on what you can't control—the outcomes, results, points, or goals scored. Refocus, instead, on believing in the following:

- Believe in yourself, as well as your team and staff. You have skills, strategies, and enough talent to perform well. Simply show up at your event and believe that you can demonstrate your current level of expertise. Believe that you are in a position where the best will happen. Expect to have fun and enjoy the process. Believe you will be better because of the experience.
- Believe in your teammates or partners. Believe that they, too, are willing to do all they can to make the most of a situation. Have discussions in the group about commitment and desire, with regard to going all-out and giving your best. Believe that you are there for each other, and when the going gets tough, you're willing to even bleed for each other.
- Believe that your coaches and leaders have the same goals and desires as you and the team, and will work endlessly to give of themselves and do all that's needed in order for everyone to experience their full potential.
- Believe that achievement is yours, when you believe all of the aforementioned. Expect to achieve higher levels of performance. Believe you will have a great experience and terrific season, as you put yourself and your teammates and coworkers in position to be the best all of you can be.

- Believe in the need to *start doing* that which you're not doing, in order to strengthen your belief in yourself. What do you need to *stop doing* that you are doing, in order to strengthen your belief in yourself?

According to American physician and psychologist John Lilly, "beliefs are limits to be examined and transcended." The ancient Chinese book, *Tao Te Ching*, teaches us that "evolved individuals have no fixed minds." Examine the ways your mind is fixed and implement change, using the following affirmations:

What I believe, I receive.

When I believe "I can," it's self-direction not self-deception.

When I act "as if," I get a lift.

My potential is unlimited. I believe this.

William James, the brilliant American philosopher, once said that "human beings, by changing the inner beliefs of their minds, can change the outer aspects of their lives."

COMPETITIVENESS: Playing With Hair on Fire

Getting to the final four was not expected. In our culture, we never show up to win, because the outcomes cannot be controlled, and focusing on winning will make you tense and tight. In our culture, we show up to simply compete by controlling all the little things brilliantly, such as diving for the 50/50 ball and tenacious defense. We did this and let the results take care of themselves. We competed like crazy, with our hair on fire.

—Cindy Timchal, Head Women's Lacrosse Coach, United States Naval Academy

Coach Timchal had seven consecutive national championship lacrosse teams at the University of Maryland. Currently on the staff at the U.S Naval Academy, Cindy asked me to consult with her and put into place a similar strong, competitive culture, as we had done in Maryland. And compete they did.

Unranked from the start of the season, Navy executed the little things brilliantly and marched into the final four, beating highly ranked Loyola, Penn, and two-time national champions University of North Carolina on UNC's home field—simply, as Cindy would say, "by competing like crazy." With guts and relentless play, Navy never gave up and never gave their opponent permission to interfere with their mission, which was to stay competitive and play with "heart from the start," a mantra I developed as part of this culture of fierce warriors. They didn't win the championship, but they were champions, because they won the day.

Steve Kerr's Golden State Warriors took a similar path during their 2014-15 season. One of the Warriors core values is competitiveness. This element came into focus during the NBA Finals, when they were down two games to one, and playing Game 4 on the Cleveland Cavaliers' home court. The media blitz was out of control, going off about how this was a "must-win" game, do or die. All focus was on the uncontrolled outcome, building enormous pressure and angst that certainly would detract from playing their best.

On an afternoon stroll on the streets of Cleveland prior to the game, Steve called to talk with me about how they might get a better perspective on this highly emotionally packed situation. The following is what I suggested to Coach Kerr:

> *The difference between the really good teams and those who are extraordinary is simply that when a good team shows up, their focus is on the outcomes and results and stats, and they feel they must win the championship to justify their greatness. When this situation occurs, they get tight, tense, and tentative, trying to control what they can't. As a result, their confidence diminishes, and their performance suffers.*
>
> *The truly extraordinary teams show up to compete and Win the Day. A factor they can control. They then feel relaxed, and are calm and focused. As a result, their confidence rises (everyone is confident, when they can control something), and their performance soars. Competitiveness for the Warriors is crashing the*

boards, sprinting the lanes, boxing out, diving for the 50/50 ball, and playing in-your-face defense, as well as all of the other ways that the Warriors compete. It is the belief that when athletes execute these details, the results take care of themselves.

Then, I gave Steve an appropriate affirmation for the team to use: when we compete, we are difficult to beat. You guys did this all season long, so I ask you, why change this, just because it's the playoffs? Nothing gargantuan is needed now...You simply need to execute the little essential absolutes brilliantly, rather than the big brilliant things marginally and that's a way to Win the Day.

Kerr is brilliant, and he knew all of this. Yet, like most people, he needed the reminder, amid all the media chaos. His humble, authentic response was: "It's exactly what I needed to hear, Jerry. I will use your advice and give it to the team to help them relax and compete, as well as have fun controlling what they can. Thanks so much for this wonderful advice." The Warriors convincingly handled the Cavs that evening. In a follow-up call, Steve mentioned how his boys "broke the code in game four. We are back to being us." They rode this wave to winning the NBA Championship in his first year as head coach.

According to former UCLA men's basketball coach John Wooden, competitiveness is simply a process, rather than a product, like results or outcomes. Otherwise, he says, you become emotionally tight and mentally weak.

Coach Wooden says, "I never mentioned winning or victory … never referred to beating an opponent." He would strongly urge his guys to strive for the satisfaction that "always comes from knowing you did the best you could to become the best of which you are capable." He emphasized effort, never the final score, as a measure of an athlete's competitiveness.

Head coach Pete Carroll of the NFL's Seattle Seahawks is an extraordinary leader, who has a similar philosophy to coach Wooden about competitiveness. To him, it's not about beating others. It is about pushing yourselves by identifying and committing to execute all the little things. Quin Snyder, head coach of the NBA Utah Jazz, refers to these little things as the "essential absolutes." Carroll intimates how counterproductive it is to focus on results. "We don't talk about championships," he says. "We talk about performing our best."

Corepics VOF/Shutterstock.com

Competitiveness is simply a process, rather than a product, like results or outcomes.

I once asked Carroll about his sense of competitiveness, and he replied, "I compete at everything." That seems to be the essence of his system. He mentioned how the culture is all about the relentless, tireless pursuit for achieving the competitive edge, in practice and games alike.

The University of North Carolina's women's soccer coach Anson Dorrance, winner of 22 NCAA championships, talks about the defining aspect of his extraordinary program. He told me, "The *competitive cauldron* is the pinnacle of our program … it fosters a quality we can all possess and control. It is governed by self-discipline and desire." It's how they Win the Day.

Cindy Timchall's women's lacrosse practice at the United States Naval Academy is highly competitive. When you watch her team practice, it has all the energy and emotion of a championship game. Like Anson's program, Navy's practice drills are designed to mimic big games by enhancing a competitive nature. Yet, Cindy tells me there is much joy in these sessions, along with much pain. She calls this "coaching it up" by modeling in practice, what it will take to be champions … now! The team's favorite drill is called "next goal wins." Try this with your team, and watch how they turn up the competitive heat.

One of my favorite messages to give my teams is one I learned from Sun-Tzu's oft-quoted book, *The Art of War*—"The war is won, before the battle begins." You accomplish this victory by having a strong commitment before the game to being competitive, focusing on the little things, and executing them brilliantly. I love to remind the coaches and athletes that the Latin root of "compete" is to "seek together" our individual and collective greatness by controlling what we can. How different this is from the word "competition," which means to "compete against."

Implementation

To help my teams infuse the core value of competitiveness into their culture, I invite them to identify their top 10 controllable little things that, when performed well, enable them to compete at their highest level. Since these "little things" vary by the position you play in sports, like soccer, lacrosse, field hockey, and football, I will ask them to gather in groups by position. For example, in lacrosse, there will be defenders, middies, and attackers. In sports like tennis, golf, and track, I will individualize the exercise to each athlete. Some of the absolutes will be universally appropriate, while others will be more personalized.

When all of this is completed, we ask the athletes to promise that they will execute these top 10 ideas, along with the other promises (see the segment on Win the Game, Win the Day). Collectively, all of these promises become our cultural definition of what we mean by competitiveness. I then ask the coaches to be sure to define success, not by the scoreboard, but by how proficient and effective the athletes are in being competitive, in demonstrating the promises attendant to this essential core value. I then have the coaches reward the athletes for achieving these little things. It's how they Win the Day.

The following strong, affirmative action plan could be an awesome banner for your culture: On this team, we compete like crazy, with our hair on fire. When we compete, we're difficult to beat.

FEARLESSNESS: Feel Free and Fly

You play good teams, so they can tell you where you need repairs. It has always been my philosophy to schedule losses. Nothing galvanizes a team like being beaten.

—Anson Dorrance, Head Women's Soccer Coach, University of North Carolina

Anson and his fearless warriors visited the West coast recently to compete against two very, very good teams in Santa Clara and at Stanford. The Tarheels lost both contests. Thinking he would be discouraged, I gave him a call—we're friends—to hear his take on the weekend results. His response was typical Anson, who has a positive spin (see the segment on the value of positivity) on everything. I quoted his aforementioned words to him. Remember his astute, insightful words the next time you're afraid of losing or feeling badly, after you do lose. To Win the Day cultures, losses, setbacks, errors, and mistakes are opportunities to learn, grow, correct weaknesses, and be a better team because of them.

One point that I emphasize to coaches and athletes is that fear is the greatest obstacle to all high-level performance and competitive problems. Fear tells me that a coach, athlete, or entire team is too focused on outcomes and results. In a Win the Day culture, we focus on just that … Win the Day by focusing on what we can control (previously discussed in Part I). Understand that fear definitely weakens you. Your muscles tighten up, cutting off sufficient oxygen, and as a result, makes it difficult to be fluid. It also inhibits the body's ability to execute its innate intelligence, creating poor performances. In addition, fear interferes with your natural ability to focus, relax, and be mindful about the task at hand.

Implementation

In the Win the Day culture, we strive to create mentally and emotionally safe environments (see the segment on the power of environment in the relationship game), free of fear over failure, mistakes, messing up, being ridiculed, or insulted. I teach coaches how to implement such an environment to help athletes get beyond this unnecessary, paralyzing fear. The following is how I do it: I offer the athletes the chance to practice being *brave*. In his inspirational book on Native American wisdom, *The Lakota Way*, Joseph Marshall III discusses how "being brave is having or displaying courage during hardship,

cheapbooks/Shutterstock.com

Fear is the greatest obstacle to all high-level performance and competitive problems.

or being strong in the face of pain and uncertainty." His suggestion for implementing bravery is to identify someone who is brave and basically imitate their behaviors. If you follow long enough, you'll learn to be fearless and have the courage to raise your level. I have used his strategy successfully from the moment I learned it from him.

In addition to this, the following steps will help you to guide your athletes toward being brave and fearless:

- I tell them about the ancient Buddhist expression: The arrow that hits the bullseye is the result of 100 misses.
- Failure is our greatest teacher. Share your personal failures with your athletes, how you learned from them, and became better for the experience. For example, I disclose how several of my books were rejected several times by publishers, yet I learned and rewrote those books, which subsequently became bestsellers.
- Ask those you lead the following three questions, after a loss or setback:
  ✓ What went well?
  ✓ What needs work? (avoid what went wrong—it's reactive, not proactive)
  ✓ Why are we a better team, athletes, culture because of that failure?
- I intend to read the Anson quote that opened this segment to all my teams going forward, when they experience a setback.

Now that our environment begins to feel safe, and fear is mitigated, I tell the team: There is only ONE decision to make. Do you want to feel *fear* or do you want to feel *free*? Of course, everyone desires the latter. Being free of worry, fear, anxiety, and stress enables you to take it to a new level.

To further help you release the fear, you should remember that you should never judge an outcome. People are too quick to get down on themselves after a loss. What did Anson say? Last year while I was working with the Stanford University's women's lacrosse team, the athletes were judging our two losses to the University of Colorado as bad, awful, crushing. I subsequently told them in our meeting—don't judge this. Then, we answered the aforementioned three questions, and I said, we'll meet them again—and we did, in the finals of the newly formed PAC-12 Conference on CU's home field. We crushed them 15-6, as we let go of all fear and simply focused on how to be free.

Another viable other idea I have for lessening fear in your culture is to remember the RIVER effect, the LUV acronym, and the Oneness Rule, all of which were previously discussed. When athletes feel the love, their fear evaporates. In fact, fear never exists, when there is love.

According to Taoist thought, approaching fear in this way is aligned with the principle of *Wu Wei,* a way of working with fear by blending with its own force. *Wu Wei* is effortless action, whereby you accept the natural way (it's natural to have fear) and exert the least amount of energy possible, when faced with such a situation. Don't fight fear or try to run away from it. Listen to its message, so you can make adjustments and be free.

Realize, as well, that sometimes fear is not fear, but an obsession with outcomes that cannot be controlled. Therefore, remember this: *FEAR* stands for *False Evidence Appearing Real.* If you feel you are in danger, ask yourself, why you feel that way? Have you prepared well? Do you have all the information you need? Are you out of your comfort zone? Assess the situation and decide what to do. To help you gain a perspective on your fear, when it looms large, I suggest remembering the wise words of renowned American singer-songwriter Bob Dylan: "What looks large from a distance, close up ain't never that big."

It never feels good to lose, experience setbacks, make mistakes, or fail. Having had much failure in my life, I notice that although it may cause disappointment at the time, all that I am today is the result of learning from such experiences. The Win the Day culture understands that, in this way, when we lose, we also win.

The other side of every fear is freedom.

—Alan Watts, British-American Author and Philosopher

GRIT: Hanging Tough, Playing Rough

At various points, in big ways and small, we get knocked down.

If we stay down, grit loses. If we get up, grit prevails.

—Angela Duckworth, American Psychologist and Author

Perhaps, more than any other characteristic of successful people is the quality of having grit. Every one of the 115 champion team cultures that I've been associated with has demonstrated grit. Angela Duckworth's classic book, *Grit: The Power of Passion and Perseverance*, relates to athletics and overall performance. *Grit* is the paragon of this genre. I highly recommend you read her acclaimed book to obtain the best handle on this essential core value. Right from the outset, she explains that "highly successful people give a ferocious determination ... they were unusually resilient and hardworking ... they knew in a very deep way what it was they wanted. It was this combination of passion and perseverance that made high achievers special. In a word, they had grit."

As a competitive distance runner for many years, I admired the mentality of the great American middle- and long-distance runner Steve Prefontaine. I still remember his words prior to a big race, when he said, and I paraphrase, "they may beat me, but they'll have to bleed to do it." That is grit.

In her book, Angela tells the story about the Grammy Award-winning actor Will Smith and his ridiculous work ethic, his grit. He explains it this way: "if we get on a treadmill together, two things could happen: you're getting off first, or I'm going to die. It's that simple."

Bob Hansen head coach of the Middlebury College men's tennis program tells a story about the grit of one of his athletes. It was spring break, he had a job, he practiced his tennis yet still turned up the volume of life by taking a simple "breather class" and still spent 24 hours writing a paper for his project. According to Bob, he was an "all-in" guy, wanting to get the most from himself. This is grit.

In the culture of UNC head women's soccer coach Anson Dorrance, grit is related to character, real personal character is what he calls it. Included in such character traits are self-discipline, competitive fire, and self-belief, as well as love for the ball and love for the game, watching or playing it. He loves Duckworth's Grit Test (included in her book) and requires all his athletes to take it to determine who has grit and to teach them, through such a test, the elements that make up grit. Like Anson, I believe that being mindful of what grit truly is, raises the possibility that you can develop it within yourself. I also believe that if you have passion and perseverance, you demonstrate grit. On the other hand, these qualities cannot be legislated by you, the coach. The athlete must want to have grit.

Knowing that Angela Duckworth visited the Seahawks' training camp, I brought up the element of grit in my conversation with head Seahawks' coach Pete Carroll. He agreed that it was about passion, perseverance, and, he added, the eagerness to "hang tough." He told me how they look for guys who have grit. It's the mindset that they'll always succeed, that they have something to prove. "We look for their resilience, not letting setbacks hold them back. We're not going to be thrown off by challenges and hurdles." It's an attitude he calls grit.

In the Win the Day culture, we never give up, we never fear failure, we never lose confidence, and we never let an opponent defeat our spirits (see Part I). USNA's women's lacrosse coach Cindy Timchal's teams are the epitome of grit. In a recent conversation, she admitted to me that our work together on grit was the one key factor in getting them to the women's lacrosse final four last year. Return to the section on "Win the Game or Win the Day" and implement the same ideas that Cindy is referring to with your team. This effort will help build grit.

Legendary NFL coach Bill Walsh of the San Francisco 49'ers had a strong conviction about his guys being "gritty." He referred to it as being resilient (see the segment on the core value of resilience). In his words, "to succeed you must fail, which is part and parcel of pursuing and achieving very ambitious goals." I remember when his team was on an eight-game losing streak, early on in his tenure, with the Niners. After a dark, dismal period, rather than give up, he discovered something inside (grit) that helped the team to keep fighting regardless of their record. The next season the 49ers won the Super Bowl.

While so many coaches and athletes seem to think that greatness is the result of talent, I refuse to accept this myth. Believing it is talent lets you off the hook—"I don't have the talent, so that's why my team is not great." It becomes an excuse to not work hard. From my experience with all of the championship teams with whom I've had the opportunity to work, as well as those championship teams of the coaches throughout this book, I've observed that a majority of them won with grit, not with talent alone. When I was a competitive athlete, I had less talent than many, but few, if anyone, could outwork me.

Implementation

Way of Champions teaches how to Win the Day, which is built on a bedrock of grit. The book you're reading at this moment is designed to teach you much of what you need to know about grit. The core values presented throughout are the foundational building blocks of grit: always compete, never give up, be all you can be, use positive self-talk, persevere, have passion, and demand more from yourself. Remember this—when you demonstrate grit, you enhance the grit in others, which, in turn, feeds back into your own grit. It's a contagious, never ending cycle.

If you asked me, "Jerry, how can I build grit in myself and my athletes?" my answer would be, attend to all of the aforementioned factors and connect with your "WHY." Why have grit? If your answer to WHY is that grit helps you to give to others; to make a difference; to create profound, lasting change; to connect with others; to be a happier person; to do what matters … your grit factor will rise exponentially.

It seems appropriate that this segment is concluded where it began, quoting the expertise of Angela Duckworth's book *Grit:*

> *I think the questions on the grit scale about not letting setbacks disappoint you, finishing what you begin, doing things with focus, I think those are the things I would hope for, for all our children.*

LOVE: Greatest Success Strategy of All

It takes a number of critical factors to win an NBA championship ... talent, creativity, intelligence, toughness, and luck. But, if a team doesn't have the most essential ingredient—LOVE—none of those factors matter.

—Phil Jackson, Former NBA Head Coach (Chicago Bulls and Los Angeles Lakers)

Some of the following you will find familiar. Repeating what was said in the section on the relationship game is intentional and useful. Repetition with variation is the mother of learning and the father of absorption, as well. In reality, you can't hear too much about, as Phil noted in the introductory quote, the most essential ingredient of a championship culture.

Grambling State football coach Eddie Robinson claimed that the secret to his success was love. Coaching is a profession of love. You can't coach athletes, unless you love them. When you do, you Win the Day.

When legendary UCLA basketball coach John Wooden retired, one reporter asked him about his extraordinary success that hasn't been matched to this day. It didn't take but a second for Wooden to reply: "There was a lot of love in my coaching."

The world's most successful women's soccer coach, Anson Dorrance of the University of North Carolina women's soccer dynasty, in a recent conversation together, talked about the importance of love as a core value in his championship culture. "We care about each other as teammates and as human beings." In his classic book, *The Vision of a Champion*, he points out how his athletes become non-judgmental, inclusive friends, who embrace each other in love, because of their sense of humanity, with no elitist separation by academics or social class, race, religion, or sexual preferences. This is one way the athletes Win the Day.

Working with Cindy Timchal, women's lacrosse coach with the most wins of all time, and her University of Maryland national championship teams, the value of love was palpable. Prior to every practice and game, we'd come together in a team circle, symbolic of being one heart, and one soul, and chant "we come together, we win together, we lose together, we compete together, we love each other." As Cindy so aptly noted, "I still believe that our affirmation of love verbally translated into how we gave our hearts physically and emotionally to the culture that won seven consecutive national championships." Twenty years removed, Cindy and I still remain friends, who maintain the love we nurtured, which impacts all of the work we do for so many others in life. That mantra was an affirmation to Win the Day. It also demonstrated caring and connections within the whole culture.

Over the years, I have grown and evolved as a coach. It's my love for my work, as well as the cultures that employ me, that I attribute to my success. This love for others tears down barriers, rips off masks, and helps me to connect deeply with athletes and coaches. It is this genuine and authentic love and connection that I believe is responsible for creating loyalty to the culture, inspiring athletes to "go the distance," and empowering them to be mentally strong. The core value of *love* is perhaps the most extraordinary success strategy.

It has been said athletes really don't care about how much you know; they just want to know how much you care. Yet, at times, we all feel frustrated, annoyed, disappointed, and turned off by some of our athletes. It's easy to love the awesome ones, who do everything perfectly well. On the other hand, we must love them all, if we wish to be effective.

While we don't have to like their behaviors, we can find a place in our hearts to love them for who they are: human beings, just like us. Their intentions are often pure, but fear, insecurity, immaturity, and confusion cloud the mission of the culture. The real challenge in creating a championship culture is to coach these difficult athletes to places they've never been, but crave, through genuine caring, connection, and love.

Laszlo Szirtesi/Shutterstock.com

While coaches don't have to like the behaviors of all of their athletes, they can find a place in their hearts to love them for who they are—human beings, just like them.

Implementation

I was told by another coach that love is not a commodity; it's a capacity. I took this observation to mean that love is the capacity to connect and care. At my annual transformative coaching conferences, I offer coaches simple, yet powerful, ways to connect and care and love. I tell them to fight for the athletes' heart. To do this, I suggest they catch the athletes doing something right.

Jenn Cook, former assistant women's lacrosse coach at the University of North Carolina (now the associate head women's lacrosse coach at Princeton University), blew her whistle every time one of the girls made a mistake. Jenn was getting nowhere with this player. When I gave her this new strategy, she implemented it for three days. On the fourth day, as she entered her office, she was greeted with a bouquet of roses with a note: "Thanks coach. These last few days have been the best days at practice in three years." This athlete transformed before our eyes, because of the love she felt each day from her coach, who now coached with a "whistle of love." She won the day.

Another suggestion I often make is asking others to liberally use my "oneness rule." Simply implemented, you and your staff choose one athlete, give them one positive comment, and do this one day at a time. It's infectious, and I notice that everyone who tries this can't stop at one. They break the code.

In this electronic age, I find it effective to use my devices to email or text my teams and individual athletes about something positive that I notice. I do this regularly, and I usually get lots of love in return.

Finally, for now, try the magic acronym, L.U.V. (love) to win the hearts of your athletes. L is for listen, the most powerful skill in your leadership toolbox. U is for understanding by asking questions that show interest in others as people. V is to validate, when their responses to your questions are statements, demonstrating positive reactions and commendable thoughts and ideas.

Sun-Tzu, in his ancient classic book, *The Art of War*, emphasizes the importance of love for success. He strongly encourages Taoist leaders and generals to take care of the troops, as they would take care of a child who was loved. He says that by loving others, the chances of victory are greatly enhanced.

Nobel Peace Prize winner Mother Teresa's words on the value of love say it all: "When we come face to face with God, we are going to be judged on how much we loved." And how often we won the day.

Finally, I leave you with some refreshing new thoughts about love from my last conversation with Missy Foote, the iconic Middlebury College women's lacrosse coach and winner of four national championships, who so beautifully stated:

> *"It's really all about LOVE, isn't it? For many years, I carried with me in my coaching clipboard (and now in my wallet) a printed, laminated copy of the Irish proverb, 'It is in the shelter of each other that the people live' to remind me that our love shelters our family and friends. As a coach and a servant leader, my obligation was to help a group of individuals come together to be*

the best they could be. It wasn't until I realized, however, that the ONLY way to help people reach their potential was through love and compassion that I became a better coach. I hope my players feel that I loved them, because I did."

MINDFULNESS: Dwelling in the Simple Present

If your mind is empty, it is always ready for anything; it is open to everything. In the beginner's mind, there are many possibilities; in the expert's mind, there are few.

—Shunryu Suzuki, Zen Buddhist Monk and Author

Head Coach Steve Kerr of the three-time World Champion Golden State Warriors knows about an empty, beginner's mind. While it's easy to put him in the role of expert, as the head coach of an NBA team, he remains wide open to anything. In fact, a huge part of his success in life can be attributed to his eagerness to "pick the brains" of others and learn from them, what he must know to be a better coach.

In all my conversations with Steve, I get a deep sense of his humble, mindful beginner's mind, coupled with his willingness to say "I don't know," leaving the door wide open for me to enter and contribute my opinions on his concerns. It is no wonder that one of the Warrior's four core values is mindfulness, mindful of the right way to do things.

I vividly remember an email exchange Steve and I had during the playoff season, when he had a question about a competitive issue. His humble, beginner's mind, open-hearted, mindful response to me was: "Thanks Jerry. It's exactly what I needed to hear. I need to use your advice and help our team to relax, be mindful, and enjoy the competition." And mindful the Warriors were on their way to the first of three championships in four years.

Of course, one of Steve Kerr's mentors happened to be Phil Jackson, the master of using mindful meditation with his Bulls and Lakers teams, on his way to winning a collective 11 championship rings. In Phil's book by the same name, *Eleven Rings: The Soul of Success*, he devotes several detailed pages on his thoughts about and use of the approach, detailed in Shunryu Suzuki's renowned book, *Zen Mind, Beginner's Mind*, to his team's performance.

To help his players on both teams to quiet the chatter of their minds and focus on the competitive nature of the game, he introduced both teams to the concept of mindfulness meditation, based on the Zen practice he learned years ago. He would get the players to sit in a room for ten or so minutes together. He called it "the warrior room." He wasn't trying to make them into Buddhist monks; it was to bring them close and bonded at the heart.

All of the athletes who took part in this voluntary exercise loved it. It was a special, unified group, who were, in the words of Vietnamese Buddhist monk, Thich Nhat Hanh "dwelling happily in the present moment," with quiet, simple, and clear minds. Jackson found through such practice that when athletes marinate themselves fully in the moment, they develop a deeper, stronger awareness (mindfulness) of what's happening right now, in the present moment. And, in Jackson's words, this "leads to a greater sense of oneness, the essence of teamwork."

The following is an inspirational story about mindfulness meditation. During the Chinese cultural revolution during the 1960's, Chinese pianist and composer Liu Shih-Kun was incarcerated for six years in prison, with no piano, and no paper to write on. Before entering his isolated solitary confinement, he was brutally worked over by one of the Red Guards, cracking bones in his arms. During his incarceration he "practiced" his music in his head, mindfully visualizing himself playing at a high level over and over. He even composed a concerto and kept it memorized. In 1973, following his release from jail, Liu played before his peers and was deemed to be even better than before he went to prison. Thus, the power of mindfulness meditation.

In fact, my Way of Champions approach, which is designed to help others to Win the Day, recommends using mindfulness training with all coaches, teams, and athletes. As such, it is important that you understand how mindfulness training is a viable tool for living, whether on the court, at work, or at home. I incorporate a meditation practice into my daily life, as part of my Win the Day program (see epilogue).

In my work with highly functional high school, collegiate, and professional athletic teams and coaches, I train them to use meditation prior to practice and games. This undertaking helps them to get more out of their practice sessions, as well as be more centered and focused on executing the game plan more effectively. This consistent practice of mindful meditation is exactly what was used by the Taoist warrior, who sought to "settle" his mind for what became an undisturbed performance. I also encourage individual athletes to consider practicing meditation each night for five minutes, after brushing their teeth, before going to bed.

Implementation

There is an ancient Taoist proverb that states: "If you know the art of breathing, you have the strength of 10 tigers."

Over the years, I have trained thousands of coaches and athletes to have tiger strength, using a 2500-year-old form of Buddhist meditation called Vipassana, a Pali word that, when translated, means insight. This meditation practice relies on the awareness that breathing is happening and using the breath as a focal point to quiet what Buddhists call the "monkey mind."

This meditative state of mind, this still point, is a sacred space that raises awareness, makes movement effortless, and confidence more robust. It helps you to find balance and keep it on your lives. It is a source of positive energy and keeps you connected to your cultural mission, Win the Day. It has a direct, positive influence on your culture and overall effectiveness, when practiced by you, your team, and athletes. It also contributes to higher more satisfying levels of performance.

KieferPix/Shutterstock.com

Mindfulness training is a viable tool for living, whether on the court, at work, or at home.

If you're ready to engage in this meditation practice, begin with your eyes closed, in a quiet place, free from interference. Sit comfortably in a chair, with your back straight and your feet on the floor. Drop your arms into your lap. Next, adhere to the following:

- Begin by taking three deep, controlled breaths, holding the oxygen in your lungs for three seconds, before you exhale. Notice how this procedure as an instant effect on your body and mind, relaxing you immediately. Then, stop and return to normal breathing.
- Simply notice that breathing is happening. Watch it come in and go out. Do not control its natural flow, other than to have it go through your nostrils.
- When your mind wanders—and it will—simply acknowledge it and direct it back by saying, "wandering, come back." Don't be concerned about the wandering: it's natural. In fact, the act of being aware of the wandering and bringing your attention back to the breath actually helps you to develop strong attention skills, when performing, coaching, or competing in everyday life. It develops what is called meta-attention. As such, wandering is an integral aspect to the full meditation practice.
- Do this "breath watching" for about eight minutes, then switch gears, and begin to visualize by feeling yourself being how you wish to be at work, performing, coaching, competing, parenting, writing … whatever it is that you do. Visualize for about four minutes.
- Following your visualization, recite a few short, positive affirmations that nurture and support your visualizations. Unlike visualizations, which involve

fizkes/Shutterstock.com

Mindfulness is about waking up to the present moment to experience the vitality of life and do that on a more consistent basis.

how you feel and what you see, these strong statements influence what you say and, more importantly, how you think. Not only do thoughts strengthen or weaken you, they also determine the direction in which you go. Affirmations are spiritual gems that keep you on the path to coach with heart. Write them out on indcx cards and, as you recite them, feel the words, as if they are real and happening now.

You may have noticed that animals instinctively know and use a method of stillness in nature. They all meditate. Observe the heron poised motionless on one leg, the monkey climbing to the uppermost branch, the snake basking in the warmth of the summer sun, or the cat lying on a pillow, its eyes focused on a small object. Such stillness prepares the inner environment for a deep, peaceful *meditative* state.

With reference to helping his athletes foster team cohesion and gain a sense of unity, Phil Jackson applauds the value of mindfulness meditation in facilitating them to break out of their me-oriented attitudes and gives them the opportunity to consider going to a more we-orientation.

In so doing, in his brilliant book, referenced earlier, *Eleven Rings: The Soul of Success*, Jackson quotes the 13th century Japanese Buddhist priest and teacher Nichiren:

> *If the spirit of many in body, but one in mind, prevails among the people, they will achieve all their goals; whereas if one in body, but different in mind, they achieve nothing remarkable.*

Tying all this together, it is important to point out that mindfulness is about waking up to the present moment to experience the vitality of life and do that on a more consistent basis. It can help you to see clearly and act more appropriately, when it comes to being the best you can be. (The Chinese symbols for *mindfulness*, when translated, mean "music from the heart as we become fully awakened with all of our sensory perceptions.")

Mindfulness has strong implications for your actions, performance, and decisions in all the arenas of athletics. In his book, *The Mindful Athlete*, renowned mindfulness teacher who works with a number of pro basketball athletes and teams George Mumford states that "pure performance starts with the mind. What's in and on your mind determines how well you perform." In Buddhism, you learn about the "monkey mind," which was discussed earlier. In reality, this scattered focus can be tamed to stay in the here and now through a more *mindful* approach.

While the notion of mindfulness is closely aligned with the roots of ancient Buddhist teaching, it is also a powerful way to practice being awake and aware of thoughts and actions, as they appear in the present moment. (It is actually a very simple concept of knowing what you are doing, as well as how you are doing it and why, while understanding how your actions influence others in a profound way to practice mindfulness.)

Its essence is universal, and you need not be a Zen Buddhist monk, sitting Zazen on a mountaintop, to practice being aware and present. Mindfulness has actually become profoundly relevant in mainstream America, being embraced by hospitals helping patients to heal, military groups wanting to focus, educational systems hoping to facilitate learning, musicians wishing to be more present, and actors trying to stay in the moment. So can we all.

PERSEVERANCE: Enduring Effort, Consistent Strength

Imagine the comfort knowing that by never giving up, you will have lived life to the fullest...such peace of mind is often reward enough.

—Bill Bradley, All Star NBA Player, New York Knicks

In the Win the Day philosophy, our athletic goals are reached each day, one day at a time, not by our strength or talents but by the core value *perseverance.* I'm not the most scholarly, brilliant writer, but I never quit. It's frustrating and often discouraging, if not disappointing, when my book proposals get rejected. In fact, my best-selling book, *Thinking Body, Dancing Mind*, was rejected for publication 13 times, before I found someone who believed in it. After the first five refusals, I almost quit ... gave up. I'm happy I didn't, because it is now printed in many languages throughout the world. Furthermore, after 28 years of it being published, I still collect a healthy check for royalties twice a year. As I write these words today, my agent has not found a publisher. On the other hand, I persevere and go forward, knowing that some lucky publisher will find it. Obviously, it has a home ... you're holding it.

Implementation

What helps me persevere in these challenging situations, and this factor may be true for you, as well, is the passion and love I have for my work, my intention to change the status quo in sports, and my mission to make a difference in your life. Perseverance is also tied to the hip of grit, which was discussed previously. I have grit … I always get up, when I'm knocked down.

To persevere, you need purpose, resilience, tenacity, and a growth mindset. In the words of renowned Irish playwright George Bernard Shaw, I "dream things that never were and ask why not?" It helps to develop a ferocious determination, as you keep putting one foot in front of the other. But the bottom line is this: without passion, there is no way to persevere.

When you follow your heart, your deepest love and desire, you will meet the caravan coming in a different direction that has all you need to continue. When you follow your passion, the universe will open doors, where there were only walls. The point is that you need passion if you hope to persevere.

In his beautiful, brilliantly written simple fable, *The Alchemist*, Brazilian novelist Paulo Coelho tells the story of a young man crossing a vast wasteland on the desert and describes how he gave up just prior to the palm trees appearing on the horizon. He didn't know, like many athletes, how close he was to success.

As part of the Win the Day culture, (see Win the Game, Win the Day) you never, ever give up. It's one of your promises to yourself, your team, the staff, and your family. It is a *choice*! When you buy in to this cultural promise, there is no turning around. You must continue the journey. As such, the team is there to support, encourage, and inspire you.

While Dean Smith, Bill Walsh, and John Wooden have long since passed, their teachings about perseverance have lasted to this day and beyond. Students of theirs teach it regularly through their example. A number of athletes, such as Michael Jordan, Joe Montana, and Kareem Abdul Jabbar, continue their coaches' legacy in the "never-give-up" mindset, as demonstrated by the way they live their lives.

Coaches like Pete Carroll, Steve Kerr, and Anson Dorrance have made perseverance an integral aspect of their championship cultures. I also notice that attribute in many of their all-star athletes. For example, even though both were recently in terrible slumps, Golden State Warriors players Klay Thompson and Steph Curry never gave up and overcame the hard times. They remind me of the wisdom of the Chinese book, *I Ching*, the book of change: "The warrior accomplishes significant deeds through enduring effort in a consistent direction."

releon8211/Shutterstock.com

When you follow your passion, the universe will open doors, where there were only walls.

Staying close to the Chinese theme, the calligraphic characters the Chinese use for perseverance illustrate strength and unwavering groundedness in the spirit of the performer. When you handle suffering with a warrior's heart, eventual success will be your reward. While talent is important, know that it accounts for a mere 5 percent of most achievements. Confucius encourages us to not lose heart, until the task is complete through steadfast movement on the Win the Day path.

In his autobiography, *Win Forever*, head Seahawks coach Pete Carroll talks specifically about the power of perseverance in his life. He says that "once you have done the work to create a clear vision, it is the discipline and the effort to maintain that vision that can make it all come true … it's the diligence with which you stick to that vision that allows you to get there."

Leaning once again on the wisdom of the Native American Lakota storyteller, Joseph Marshall III, you can't truly succeed without perseverance. On the brink of extinction, the buffalo survived by persevering.

POSITIVITY: Changing Thoughts, Changing Lives

A positive attitude causes a chain reaction of positive thoughts, events, and outcomes.

It is a catalyst, and it sparks extraordinary results.

—Wade Boggs, Hall of Fame Professional Baseball Player

University of North Carolina head women's soccer coach Anson Dorrance, in a recent conversation, related to me how in his Carolina culture, "we choose to be positive. Nothing can depress or upset this powerful and positive life force … not mood swings, not even negative circumstances affect this rock. We don't whine or cause drama." The operative word in his statement is "choose." Positivity is a choice, and you control that decision.

I can attest to the universality of his words with other championship coaches I've worked with over the years. All of the Hall of Fame coaches who have contributed to this book helped their athletes Win the Day through their relentless pursuit of a strong positive environment on and off the court.

Dean Smith, former UNC head men's basketball coach, was one of these leaders who used positivity to influence his players. As a result they learned to be more confident, develop their loyalty and play tough. During time-outs of close games, he was particularly positive, with phrases like: "Have some fun," or "I love being in this situation." Whether they won or lost the game, his positivity made the athletes feel respected and their dignity upheld. In his book, *The Carolina Way*, Smith points out how "I believe strongly in positive reinforcement … we praised behavior that we wanted to see repeated."

I truly love being in the company of Bob Hansen, Middlebury College men's tennis coach. He claims that all of his championships were deeply influenced by the contagious, on-and-off-the-court environment of positivity he built during his career as a coach.

Prior to a victory that propelled them into a Final Four, the Navy women's lacrosse team needed one goal to finish off their opponent. With a free position, eight-meter shot waiting to be taken, head Middie coach Cindy Timchal looked at the shooter, during a time-out, and told her: "I know you'll score, but even if you don't, remember we will still love you." The young freshman stepped up to the hash mark and drained a rocket into the upper right-hand corner of the cage, putting her team into the championship weekend.

Implementation

In my work with Win the Day cultures, I positively encourage coaches to catch athletes doing something right. The whistle is an effective coaching and teaching tool. If you, as a coach, are a whistle-blower, and you believe that your actions are a deterrent to your athletes' forward progress, you should remember the story that was recounted in the segment on love, about Jenn Cook, assistant women's lacrosse coach at North Carolina. Her shift from blowing a whistle at an athlete's mistake to waiting for an athlete to show their greatness and then blowing the whistle completely changed the atmosphere on the playing field and beyond, for every athlete on the team.

Positivity can change a life. One small comment at the right time can direct you to your calling. You should again refer to *The Relationship Game*, where examples of the power of love in coaching were shared. You will recall the oneness rule, and the positive impact that this precept can have on each of your athletes. Personally, I will never forget how one college professor's comment had such a positive impact on my life, with just a few words. As such, you and your staff are encouraged to choose one athlete each day, once each day, and give them one positive comment for doing something right. It's easy, simple, controllable, and contagious. You could change an entire life. It happened to me.

The whistle is an effective coaching and teaching tool.

Positivity begins with your thoughts; thoughts are expressed with words; words direct your behavior. Your words can strengthen or weaken you. They have an energy all their own. The direction you go on or off one court is determined by your choice of words. The training program of the U.S. Navy Seals knows this factor to be true. They claim that positive words are one of the most important elements of success. They teach how positivity bridges the gap between where you are and where you go.

There is a well-known Native American story about the value of positivity. It is a Cherokee legendary tale and it goes basically like this:

> An old Cherokee is teaching his grandson about life. "A fight is going on inside me," he said to the boy. "It is a terrible fight and it is between two wolves. One is evil—he is anger, envy, sorrow, regret, greed, arrogance, self-pity, guilt, resentment, inferiority, lies, false pride, superiority, and ego." He continued, "The other is good—he is joy, peace, love, hope, serenity, humility, kindness, benevolence, empathy, generosity, truth, compassion, and faith. The same fight is going on in you—and inside every other person, too."
>
> The grandson thought about it for a minute and then asked his grandfather, "Which wolf will *win*?" The old Cherokee simply replied, "The one you feed."

To teach and coach the value of positivity in your culture, remember the oneness rule and the RIVER effect, previously discussed, and catch someone doing something right. In addition to that, take a page from the playbook of the U.S. Navy Seals, who make use of positive affirmations in their training. I have written about affirmations earlier and consider them to be strong statements that create positive self-direction. They are one of the cornerstones of building mentally, emotionally, and spiritually strong cultures. The Seals refer to these statements as their internal dialogue. The following is an example I recently shared with Steve Kerr during playoff time: "We are valiant brave Warriors, and we dare you to stop us. We are relentless, we are strong, we are fearless fighters."

Feel free to implement a program of affirmations impacting the inner dialogue of your athletes, using some of all of the following from my championship cultures. They are aligned with all the strategies discussed in this book, *Win the Day*.

- When we compete, we are difficult to beat.
- I use the F.A.C.T.S. to compete and let the results take care of themselves. (Fearlessness, awareness, competitiveness, thoughtfulness, selflessness … these will be thoroughly explained as you continue reading.)
- I am always confident, because I know I can execute only what I control—competing.
- I show up to simply compete and not try to control outcomes.
- All my mistakes and setbacks are actually great teachers. I learn from them and forge ahead as a better athlete and person.
- I refuse to let my fears stand in the way of my potential.
- My mission is simple: to do my best today to be the best I can be and position myself for great things to happen.

- When I make a mistake I say, "That stinks, I can do better … watch me, here I go."
- We are a tough, strong, fearless bunch of outrageous warriors, competing with the heart of a lion.
- We refuse to ever, ever give up, regardless of score, position, or opponent.
- You may defeat me on the scoreboard, but you can never beat my fearless, fighting, determined spirit.
- I am aware of the power of my influence and make it positive.
- I am the strong powerful influence I want to be.
- We dedicate our lives to each other, refusing to let anyone of us fail.
- The only way to achieve our mission and goal is to be "all-in" and attack.
- All-in brings nothing less than success. I lock the backdoors and cut off any option to retreat.
- I fully commit myself—body, mind, and spirit—to the work at hand, to the teammates I love.
- We go from "working together to beat our opponent" to "let's work together to compete like crazy, doing what we love to do."

I suggest you have your athletes choose the ones that resonate with them and put them on cards, one per card, and/or place them in the most visible way in the locker room. Read them out loud alone or in a group to reinforce their power to direct your culture.

I leave you with the following quote that brings together the importance of positivity upon your core values:

Keep your thoughts positive, because your thoughts become your words.

Keep your words positive, because your words become your behavior.

Keep your behavior positive, because your behavior becomes your habits.

Keep your habits positive, because your habits become your values.

Keep your values positive, because your values become your destiny.

— Mahatma Gandhi, Indian Social Activist and Writer

Bannafarsai_Stock/Shutterstock.com

Individual athletes are encouraged to consider practicing meditation each night for five minutes, before going to bed.

SUFFERING: Comfortable Being Uncomfortable

Suffering is caused by wishing things were other than they are.

—Gautama Buddha, Buddhist Monk, Philosopher, and Teacher

The life of an athlete or coach is not easy. More often than not, much suffering is part of the journey. In fact, it can be excruciatingly painful being forced to become uncomfortable in so many ways.

While this core value is an important aspect of the Win the Day culture, I can honestly say that few coaches considered this value, prior to my initiating a discussion with them about it. Now, all of the teams in my career can see why I call suffering a value. As such, it can be invaluable to help understand and address with the inevitable occurrence of suffering in sports.

Arguably, everyone knows that if you wish to improve, you need to suffer or become uncomfortable. By its very nature, sports, while bringing joy and satisfaction, evoke a degree of suffering in everyone. On occasion, people experience feelings of frustration, fear, grief, sadness, regret, anger, anxiety, or despair. To a degree, this situation is exactly like life as a whole, but more intense, and occurring over a shorter duration.

Of course, you may also suffer, when you experience loss, failure, setbacks, and errors. You feel pain, because your role on the team seems meaningless. In addition, there's the suffering associated with being physically injured, getting less playing time, having a reduced level of social life, and, if you're a student-athlete, being disappointed in your grades.

Much is also sacrificed, when you choose to be a coach or athlete. In that regard, soccer icon and World Cup champion Mia Hamm talks about this sacrifice: "I am a member of a team. I defer to it and sacrifice for it, because the team, not the athlete, is the ultimate champion."

Implementation

To coach other individuals on the value of suffering, I simply teach a *perspective* taken from other philosophies and cultures, as well as my own life experiences, which is how I help others embrace a new counterintuitive approach to this value. While suffering is often the gateway to enlightenment, in athletics, it is the gateway to greatness. Whenever you seek to experience higher levels of performance in any aspect of life, get prepared to suffer. On the other hand, as you leave your comfort zone, you'll begin to feel how expansive your potential truly is.

Buddhist thought tells us that we must accept suffering as a way of life; this is the first of Four Noble Truths in Zen. All greatness, awareness, and acute sensitivity are the natural outcomes of adversity and suffering. There is a wonderful story of an elite university athlete who was at death's door due to a serious ailment. Following nine months in the hospital, he recovered, and within a year, he returned to his team. His awareness, appreciation, and sensitivity enabled him to work extra hard on the field and do more than was asked of him, because he was enormously grateful to be alive. His suffering had made him a better athlete, teammate, and person, while his teammates still cut corners, only working hard, when the coaches were present. The lessons he learned from his suffering changed his entire outlook on life. Now he is called "the team Buddha."

The Win the Day athlete and coach know that in suffering—experiencing painful feelings or being uncomfortable—you begin to see the more meaningful side of athletics and life. There is wisdom in the existential experience of suffering. Deep appreciation is often the residual benefit. When you can take this stance, you not only grow, learn, blossom, and connect with your warrior within, you also experience your full human capacity.

To demonstrate my investment in the value and relevancy of suffering, I've designed my brand logo with that factor in mind. When you read the following, I hope you get a strong sense about the power of this warrior.

Sergey Edentod/Shutterstock.com

In suffering—experiencing painful feelings or being uncomfortable—you begin to see the more meaningful side of athletics and life.

My business logo, prominently displayed on the back cover of this book, is the Chinese character for *warrior*. Since there is no word for *champion* in Chinese, I use the two interchangeably. All warriors are champions and vice versa. This is a powerful, profound logo, whose meaning goes beyond simply identifying my company.

While my business logo is easily recognizable in my national network in the field of athletics, it also identifies my purpose, my belief, my way, and the culture I create. It represents the "WHY" factor of my work, which is to make a difference; to change the status quo of sports; to be a servant to others, helping them to compete and coach with heart; to enable those individuals to be something other than ordinary, as they navigate not only the game of sport, but the bigger game of life. It is a symbol for all of this, as well as my core values that drive winning in a culture of champions. I recommend that you observe this logo, as you read and study the following:

> *The Chinese character in my logo shows the warrior's arms busting out of the red box. You can also see the legs at the bottom, stretching wide open to break out of the confined box. Inside the red box, notice how all is black and white … this is myopic vision and thought. For example, functioning inside the box, when we see things as black and white, we believe that all loss is bad, soft is weak, opponents are our enemies, more is better. The real champion things outside the box … loss is our greatest teacher, soft is often strong, opponents are our partners, providing a chance to see how good we really are, and less*

is often more. Such outside-the-box thinking is emblematic of the way of the warrior and the Win the Day champion.

You will notice that when the warrior breaks out, a painful transformation occurs … things go from black and white to gray, the zone of being open, ready, and poised to battle freely, without fear. The warrior expects nothing and yet is ready for anything. They learn from those losses and become stronger as a result.

The box is red. In Chinese, the color red means transformation and fire. In life, anything that contacts fire suffers and transforms. But like all change in life, all evolvement, all greatness requires some pain, suffering, and hard work. Accordingly, the warrior, knowing this, approaches the fire, works hard, suffers, and comes out the other side transformed and able to compete at a higher level. All greatness in sports (as well as growth in life) demands that you suffer, and the results will come. The box being red also symbolizes love, passion, and heart. When you have these three ingredients present in whatever you do, you are able to persist, persevere, and believe that through all the suffering, all is possible on your personal and collective journey of discovering your greatness.

The following is my interpretation of the original serenity prayer to be used by suffering coaches and athletes. Feel free to implement it, write it out, group-text it to your team and friends, and use it when experiencing suffering:

Grant me the serenity to accept my errors, mistakes, failures and losses, pain, and suffering. Give me the courage to learn from these and change appropriately. And afford me the wisdom to forgive myself, have self-compassion, improve, and go forward.

TRUST: Bedrock of Sacred Space

Trusting is part of our higher nature. Doubting is a lower instinct.

The latter is easy to do, the former more difficult—but so much more rewarding.

—John Wooden, Former Head Men's Basketball Coach, UCLA

In the Win the Day cultures, I often talk about having the sacred space, that safe environment where you feel free to fail, mess up, and look silly. I also speak about the necessity to trust your hearts, your minds, and your bodies, having prepared them well for battle. I've been speaking about this way of trust for years, and prior to writing this section, this quote magically appeared in my reading about the Native American tradition on trust.

> *Great Mystery, teach me how to trust my heart, my mind, my intuition, my inner-knowing, the sense of my body, the blessings of my spirit. Teach me to trust these things, so that I may enter my Sacred Space and love beyond my fear, and thus walk in balance with the passing of each glorious Sun.*
>
> *—Lakota prayer*

Head women's field hockey coach at the University of Maryland, Missy Meharg, has told me that our work on trust helped influenced several of her teams to win a national championship. Our mutual friend, Cindy Timchal, the head women's lacrosse coach at USNA, claims that win or lose, trust is a non-negotiable for her teams. For Missy, trust is concern that you treat others, as you want to be treated. She agrees that it's a value developed from inside a safe, sacred space. As a coach, you can create the power of a safe environment (see The Relationship Game section in Part II).

For many Hall of Fame coaches, trust is literally the bedrock of their cultures. As such, it is maintained, when all the core values are upheld, when we hold each other accountable for that circumstance. No accountability, no trust. Trust helps you to take necessary risks, with the values being the safety net.

Phil Jackson's championship teams, the Bulls and Lakers, became great, when the players began to trust each other enough to surrender the "me" for the "we." Similar to Phil, Mike Krzyzewski, head men's basketball coach at Duke University believes that in any organization, trust must be developed among every member of the team, if success is going to be achieved.

In Bob Hansen's championship tennis teams at Middlebury College, trust is vital. On the other hand, he told me that it takes time … it's slow to develop and takes patience and perseverance. When he began at Middlebury College, he saw trust grow every year, and when it did, the team went further in the NCAA's from the round of 16 to the quarter finals, then to the semifinals, and finally to the finals—ultimately, winning it all in his fifth year. His way of building trust is through listening. "It's a way to learn about the kids, and the more I know about them, the better the culture gets." His trust is so strong in his team that he lets them decide the lineup, which empowers them. He loves to ask the question, "What do you think can make us better?" He trusts their input and implements what they say. While this strategy might not work for all of us, it's interesting that Bob won 15 championships, using his trust methodology.

During a lunch conversation with Anson Dorrance, winner of 22 national championships in women's soccer at UNC, he talked openly about the value of trust in his culture. "Jerry, it is crucial. We all must be open, transparent, and honest from the coach down to the players. We build it by being highly competitive in practice and being positive in our environment." More philosophically, former UCLA head men's basketball coach John Wooden reminds all of us how trusting is a part of our higher nature. Doubting is a lower instinct. It's easy to doubt, but trusting is more rewarding.

Famed American journalist and novelist Ernest Hemingway once said, "The best way to find out if you can trust somebody is to trust them." Many coaches, including myself, have difficulty trusting ourselves to follow the advice of this classic writer. I'm getting better at this, as I let go of my defensive Brooklyn, N.Y. upbringing, where few were trusted to be trusted, including ourselves. In my culture work with teams, I have made great strides implementing trust and developing it in the athletes by adhering to the following list of suggested steps. Perhaps, you can try these on and feel how they fit.

Implementation

- Spend more time developing caring, safe relationships with others.
- Demonstrate sincere humility.
- Begin to listen with intent.
- Involve the athletes in your system by empowering them to contribute
- Be open to learning from your athletes. My four kids at home are my best teachers.
- Make changes slowly, or resistance will grow.
- Be kind.
- Remember to catch them doing something right.
- Don't take yourself too seriously … laugh at yourself, when mistakes are made.
- Tell them you trust them … then demonstrate it.

We are now at the end of Part IV, team values, and are ready to transition to Part V, Finding Life Balance. Never forget that the values detailed in Part IV must be modeled by you, the coach, if you expect your athletes to abide by you and demonstrate these attributes in your Win the Day culture. In the words of Mahatma Gandhi, we must "be the change we want to see."

PART V

FINDING LIFE BALANCE—
Win the Day Choices

The best and safest thing is to keep a balance in your life … if you can do that, and live that way, you are really a wise man.

—Euripides, Ancient Greek Tragedian

You are almost finished with this book. At this point, you now have a "toolbox" filled with ways to build and sustain a championship culture. To better assist you in this process, Part V provides you with a compass to stay more balanced in your personal coaching life.

As such, we've come full circle from introduction to conclusion, using the True North analogy. Your future, where you go, what you do, how you do it, and why you do it will be shaped by the conscious choices you make to stay balanced in the present everyday life of coaching. I invite you to discover ways to find balance in your coaching life and to increase the power of influence you have in your leadership and coaching. When you model a Win the Day approach in your personal life, the buy-in to your cultural shifts and winning the day from your athletes will be stronger and more lasting.

It may be helpful for you to let me take you through my process in the hope of influencing you to take on the challenge. In that regard, it is important to be aware that my work and life are intricately intertwined and devoted to winning the day. *Why* I continue to work after all these years is relatively simple:

- I wish to make a difference by inspiring others to do things that inspire them, so that we all can change the world of athletics and live healthy, productive lives.
- I wish to change the status quo of leadership, athletics, and all the obsolete methodologies, being utilized by so many of us.
- I wish to serve others and empower them to believe that they can be something other than ordinary on and off the court. It's about winning the day in all aspects of life.
- I wish to master my craft and learn to be the very best version of me possible professionally and personally in my daily routines.

The focus on my "*why*" is an awesome reminder for me concerning how to establish balance in life and be more vulnerable, authentic, and genuine, leading to solid, refreshing relationships in all aspects of my life. My "*why*" is my mission, my purpose, my belief and raison d'être, what gives me meaning in all of life.

Because of my clearly defined purpose, when I embody this "*why*," I can inspire and empower others to live more fully. Because of this clarity of purpose, others buy in, not to what I do or say (they will forget what I do or say), but rather to my *why*,"…which is how I make them feel, and they never forget that. What I do and how I do it serve as the reflection, or proof, of my "*why*." What and how are the results of that "*why*." My purpose never changes, but the how and what does … as I continue to research, write, learn, and be honored to engage in efforts that illuminate such a path. It's awesome to still have others interested in reading what I write and listening to what I have to say.

Having said all this, know that for Way of Champions to continue to fulfill its "*why*" factor, may I respectfully suggest that we all do everything we can to encourage each other to *embody* these purposes in a balance of body, mind, and spirit. We must be the change we ask others to be. We must consider ways to demonstrate in our teaching process how we can be connecting, loving, giving, serving, inspiring, empowering, and affirming during the work that we do and the life we live.

Furthermore, we must embody the message by *being* the very coach, teacher, mentor, and guide that we are actually talking about, while we are teaching. If we teach our athletes to be conscious of living healthy lives and developing their full human capacity, we must model what we teach in our own lives. We need to find multiple ways to personify our "*why*," connect with others, and be the leaders we want our athletes to be. As such, we not only

SeventyFour/Shutterstock.com

Coaches must embody the message by being the very coach, teacher, mentor, and guide that they are actually talking about, while they are teaching.

disseminate important information, we actually model it, in order to help others to *feel* what it's like, when they are being led in this way.

By so doing, there will be immediate payoff, and the athletes will access the appropriate tools to achieve their greatness, which is how we empower everyone we teach. This is a level of richness to which I, myself, aspire. All in all, I am getting closer every day, after all these years. Every time I work, I try to push the boundaries of my potential, take risks, and let myself be seen, be vulnerable, and live the life I teach in body, mind, and spirit.

At times, I may preach my vision to others, but it's when I have the courage to *live* it right there in the moment that I am most effective. When we physically and emotionally embody our purpose, we begin to truly *inspire* and *empower*. More people are realizing that this is the way to stay balanced and be more effective in our process of helping and serving others. In this way, we can Win the Day.

Balanced living is my greatest challenge. I know what to do and how to do it, but it's when I stay connected to others, using my purpose or "*why*," taking the risk to be vulnerable and embody what I teach, that miracles happen, sea change occurs, work is joy, people are amazing, and I live my life in an authentic balanced way.

If I were to be asked, "Why should we work with you?" I would confidently respond that the coaching I am doing today is better than what I was doing a month ago. Furthermore, the coaching I will be doing in a month will be better than what I am doing today. This situation is because I am connected to my "*why*." At this time in life, I am the best teacher, best coach, best partner, best husband, and best dad I've ever been. I believe that my work invites more trust, respect, loyalty, creativity, optimism, connection, innovation, and love.

I pass this very personal information on to you, because I believe it will help you to understand your process more profoundly and why I offer you the following compass so that you have choices for conscious change, if you so choose. That change is how you can create balance and Win the Day in life, thus making it possible for you to inspire others to Win the Day in theirs.

This change, however, must come from within. When I state this point, I remember the ancient Buddhist story, in which a monk says to the hot dog vendor, "Make me one with everything." The hot dog vendor prepares it and gives it to the monk. The monk pays him and asks for change. The vendor then says, "Change comes from within."

In reality, I try to create a more balanced life each day in several ways. In that regard, I encourage you to find your own path of balance or take pieces of mine and apply them, accordingly. Remember that there are several routes to the same light called balance. We each have our own True North, an individual conscious compass dictated by preferences, desires, likes, and dislikes.

There is no one right way to achieving a balanced life. Rather, it is a path designed by your deepest, fondest core values that usually stand alone, yet often overlap those of others. I simply make suggestions, based on my observations and experiences from years of work to find my "sweet spot" at this time in life.

My path feels comfortable, and it is satisfying and meaningful to me. On the other hand, this is about *you*! What makes you comfortable in your own skin? What

Africa Studio/Shutterstock.com

There is no one right way to achieving a balanced life.

choices can you make to help you attain more balance and Win the Day? Be aware that this is an experiment and, like any worthwhile journey, changes in direction will happen. As long as your intention is pure, and your feet are pointed forward, you will embark on what American literature professor Joseph Campbell referred to as "the hero's journey."

When I look back on each day, I know I'm living a balanced life when I've accomplished at least seven of the following 10 items. A really awesome day is hitting it out of the park, with all 10 of these choices:

❑ Gratefulness

In the segment on gratefulness and Brother David, I talk about the exercise I give my teams who go "from grateful to great." In this instance, I start my Win the Day approach by naming seven things I'm grateful for at that moment: health, friends, work, family, mental clarity, my home, and my opportunities. All factors considered, this list could change day-to-day, as my life expands and more comes my way. I breathe the feeling of gratefulness into my heart, hold the breath for a few seconds, and do it three times. I then tell myself, "go about your day and give to others, because of all you've been given. Make my work a reflection of all I am grateful for right now." This mindset is an amazing start to a day, and if I avoid it, the difference is palpable.

❑ Exercise

I admit that I'm addicted to running and biking, and can easily lose the ability to have balance in my life. Typically, I work out in the morning and certainly before noon because getting the blood flowing early contributes to a fuller more energized, vital day. I try to get from one to two hours of exercise daily, but let's not put a time or length to this. After all, 30 minutes of cardiovascular efforts four times a week is sufficient. Initially, you should assess your level of fitness and then adjust accordingly. And remember, walking counts, as does swimming.

❑ Nutrition

Once again, I am reminding you that I do not know what's best for anyone. My nutritional choices have come about as a lifelong experiment. What I choose, when it comes to this aspect of life, is what works best for me, what feels good, and what matches my lifestyle, at my age. I am certain, however, that nutritional balance is crucial to our overall health, wellness, vibrancy, clarity, and energy, day-to-day.

I would like to note one caveat. My wife is a physician, as well as a certified clinical nutritionist. Furthermore, we have a dear friend, John Robbins, who is the author of the best-selling book, *Diet for a New America*, as well as CEO of the surging movement, the *Food Revolution Network.* You can imagine what our dinners are like, when we get together. As John would say, "I eat whatever I want."

The catch, however, is, I only want to eat an organic, plant-based diet, no dairy, no sugar, no caffeine, no alcohol. Yes, this is beyond a vegan diet. While some see this as radical, I call it winning the day; I've never, ever felt better in my life. I've been health-conscious for decades, but this is "over-the-top" health. My barometer is not how long my life will be, but how wide it is.

I am not recommending this approach for others. We all must find out what feels best for ourselves. Experiment for yourselves, but *do something*. My wife, Jan, tells her patients that food is either the best medicine or it's a slow poison. If you're an athlete and seem worried about changes to your diet (many pro and collegiate athletes are vegan), there is much to read, and it gets confusing.

John Robbins has connections with several of the best minds in the medical profession, many of whom are brilliant researchers in this controversial area. I am the beneficiary of all this wisdom through Jan and John. I simply offer this advice to help you examine your nutritional limitations, transcend them, and seek ways to create more balance in your nutritional life.

❑ Meditation

There are many avenues to explore, when it comes to the process of mediation, which is slowly becoming a household word. I refer you to the segment on value of mindfulness in Part IV of this book, if you're interested in this concept.

For me, I have a daily (almost daily) meditation practice, ranging from as little as five to 45 minutes, depending upon how my day plays out. If you only have five minutes, it would be enough to feel the positive effects of this quiet, mind-clearing session. For example, after brushing and flossing your teeth, before bedtime, take five minutes to meditate and then "hit the sack."

❑ Reading

Similar to meditation, many individuals claim that they don't have enough time to include reading in their busy day. To which I ask, do you have five minutes? Most people do. Take those minutes and read a few poems, essays, or short chapters in a book. On some days, I read for hours—usually, when it's raining on a Sunday afternoon, and nothing else is happening. Still, I maintain the balance in this regard, when I read a minimum of 5 to 10 minutes daily. It calms and relaxes me, fills my soul and enriches my brain, and gives me a good perspective on life, especially if the content has spiritual value.

❑ Strength Training

Strength training is an activity I recommend that you do two to three times per week. It feels good to pump iron and pump the blood throughout the body. In reality, to not do this on a consistent basis is to risk losing significant amounts of lean muscle mass, as you get older. My schedule is to lift three times per week, for 20 minutes a session, to maintain physical muscular balance.

❑ The RIVER

The RIVER is easy and takes a minimal amount of time. In fact, I always can Win the Day, when I baptize friends, clients, and family in the RIVER. Review the material on the RIVER in Part II, and begin to implement the suggestions for putting it into action.

❑ Affirmation

If you were a fly on my office wall, you'd see a stack of cards on my desk that I read daily. These are my self-directing affirmations that I use to keep me in position and poised for good things to happen. Go back to the segment on the value of positivity and read again about how the power of your words will help you Win the Day. Once my nervous system has been completely marinated in these words, I move forward, creating more to keep life's balance rolling forward. It takes three minutes a day to do this exercise.

❑ Relationship

One of the secrets to longevity by individuals who are centenarians is community. By nature, I tend to be introverted, filling up my emotional tanks by being alone. I make diligent efforts, however, to be with other people part of my day. I do this with clients, teams, family, and friends. Relationships (i.e., social connections) are crucial to full capacity living. How do you fill the void when it exists?

❑ Kindness

Finally, every day I look for an opportunity to extend a random act of kindness to someone, even if it's not acknowledged by that person. It just feels good to help others feel good. It doesn't take much, e.g., hold a door for someone, pick up trash on a trail, tell someone you appreciate them, etc. … you know how to do this. You just need to be mindful about doing it. You can never get out of balance by being too kind.

If you feel that this list is too much to do, add up the time commitment involved in creating such balanced living. You can do all 10 items in about an hour to an hour and a half. Imagine how balanced you'll feel, when you consistently do this. All it takes is to be mindful and create a routine. Add new items and then take some away. The key is to *give*—to yourself and to others the gift of balance. Let there be no end to your generosity. That alone helps to Win the Day. In the wise words of American author and Unitarian minister Robert Fulghum, "Live a balanced life. Learn some and think some, and draw and paint and sing and dance and play and work every day some." As such, balance in your coaching life is the essential way to Win the Day.

And so it is, with winning the day, every day. The change you experience on this journey will come from within and ripple outward to all things in your life. This quest for balance, which you can undertake, is an inner one, filled with wisdom, very private, and deeply personal. Marcel Proust, a brilliant French novelist, says that there are two methods of obtaining such wisdom—painlessly from a teacher or painfully from life. Of the two options, the latter is far superior. That said, I do not pretend to teach you wisdom. You must learn it for yourself on this Win the Day coaching journey. I simply offer you this handy, practical guide to help you stay the course, as you embark on these unchartered waters. Practice these sacred lessons of champions—lessons on mental strength, conscious leadership, and true winning the day in your sport and at work. Let this book comfort you along "the way."

Fasten your seat belt, and get ready for a fun-filled ride.

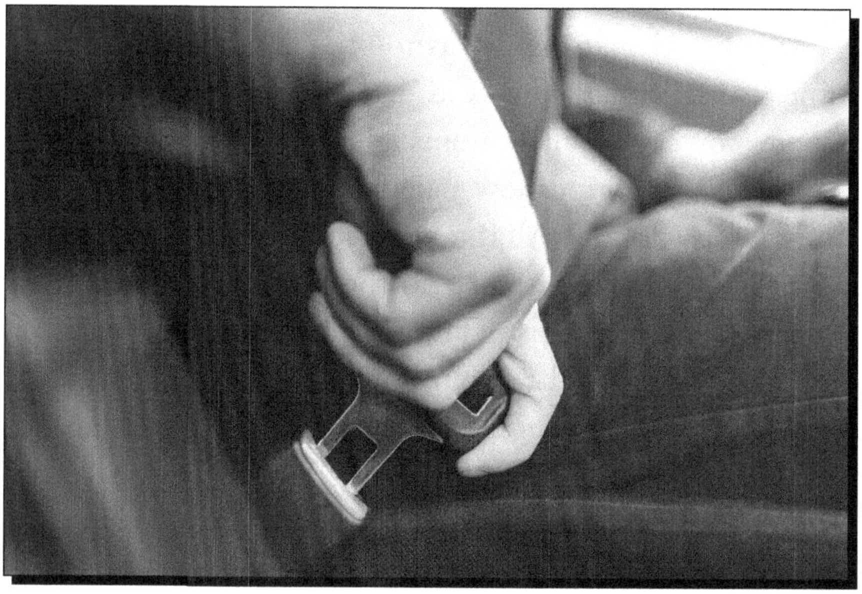

Aleksey Korchemkin/Shutterstock.com

ABOUT THE AUTHOR

While most would consider him simply a sports psychologist, Dr. Jerry Lynch is a coach, mentor, and teacher who guides and coaches athletes and parents to explore the meaning and purpose of sport as a powerful vehicle to help us understand the mental-emotional-spiritual components of the athletic game and how they apply to the bigger game called LIFE. In the process of this exploration, overall athletic performance is greatly enhanced.

Dr. Lynch has a deep calling, one where his success is not measured by "making a living" but rather by "making a difference" in the athletic and personal lives of those with whom he works. He helps others to understand how sport is a microcosmic classroom for helping athletes, coaches, and parents of sports kids develop crucial capacities to love, respect, and care for each other while simultaneously learning to enhance the spiritual elements of courage, commitment, compassion, patience, perseverance, sacrifice, integrity, trust, belief, and selflessness: the values so absolutely essential to extraordinary performance in athletics and life.

Using an unconventional approach, he combines Eastern thought, Native American tradition, Christian mysticism, and Western psychology to help coaches, parents, and athletes to create confidence, mental toughness, inspiration, and empowerment for competitive events and to better navigate the uncharted waters of sports parenting and life.

Dr. Lynch has been recognized as one of the top five in his profession nationwide. He has worked with collegiate men's and women's basketball, lacrosse, soccer, tennis, golf, and other sports at North Carolina, Duke, Maryland, California, Syracuse, Stanford, Harvard, and Middlebury and continues to work with several teams and parent groups nationally. Several of his clients have participated in various summer and winter Olympic Games. Most recently, he has established a consultancy with Steve Kerr, head coach of the World Champion Golden State Warriors. In the past 30 years alone, he has been part of 54 Final Four and 36 National Championship teams at the collegiate and professional levels.

Dr. Lynch is a well-known and in-demand public speaker at leadership, coaching, athletic, and corporate conventions. He also presents conferences, clinics, and workshops for college and high school coaches, sports parents, and athletes. He is dynamic, entertaining, motivating, provocative, and humorous, presenting topics on Peak Performance and the Way of Champions in a practical, easy-to-apply manner. Some of his presentations include keynote talks at the New Zealand National Academy of Sport, Der Deutsche Schmerztog in Germany, the National Field Hockey Coaches Association convention, the Ironman Sports Medicine Conference in Hawaii, the US Lacrosse Convention, and the NIKE/China Leadership Summit in Lanai, Hawaii.

Dr. Lynch has had extensive media interview coverage including CBS, NBC, and PBS national television, *The New York Times, The Oprah Magazine, Sports Illustrated, The Baltimore Sun, Outside* magazine, and over 50 national radio broadcasts, podcasts, and webinars.

Dr. Lynch received his doctorate in psychology from Penn State University and has done extensive post-doctoral work in the area of philosophy, Taoist and Buddhist thought, comparative religions, leadership development, and performance enhancement. He has been a national class athlete, having been a member of a national championship team and, to this day, continues to run and bike. He has coached at the high school level as well as AAU sports.

He is the author of 13 books in as many as 10 languages on coaching, leadership, spirituality of sport, warrior spirit, peak performance, and sports psychology. He has nine DVDs on the Way of the Champion, as well as two six-CD audio boxes on Performance in Athletics.

Dr. Lynch is the founder and director of Way of Champions, a performance consulting group geared toward helping others master the inner game for peak performance in athletics and develop the essential spiritual qualities so necessary for the game of life. He maintains a private practice and an extensive sports psychology consultation service for athletes, coaches, and parents around the world.

In this coming year, Jerry is excited to announce that he will be merging his business with John O'Sullivan, CEO and Director of Changing the Game Project, to form a separate nationwide program that will focus on serving the needs of youth sports parents and coaches. Using podcasts, webinars, and "in-person" clinics as platforms, their mission is to create a paradigm shift, a sea change, in how we mentor, teach, and guide these young stars as well as their parents.

Jerry is the father of four high energy, athletic children. He divides his time between his offices in Santa Cruz, California, and Boulder, Colorado, where he works and writes in the spirit of what he teaches and coaches.

CONTACT JERRY:

Jerry Lynch, PhD
C/O Way of Champions
424 Oxford Way
Santa Cruz, CA 95060
Phone: 831-234-5606
Email: wayofchampions@gmail.com
Website: wayofchampions.com

If you would like to set up a speaking engagement, workshop, or conference with Dr. Lynch, please contact his office directly via his email address only.

We would love to hear your comments, thoughts, ideas, and observations about this book. Again, contact Dr. Lynch at his email address.